PASSIVE INCOME MASTERY

DITCH THE 9-TO-5 AND UNLOCK FINANCIAL FREEDOM THROUGH ROYALTIES, STOCKS, CRYPTO, RENTALS, REITS, DROPSHIPPING, YOUTUBE, COURSES, DIGITAL PRODUCTS, AND MORE

LUCAS STERLING

TOP TIER PRESS

AF808344

© **Copyright © 2025 Top Tier Press - All rights reserved.**

Published under the author brand **Lucas Sterling**

No part of this publication may be reproduced, stored in a retrieval system, or transmitted in any form or by any means—electronic, mechanical, photocopying, recording, scanning, or otherwise—except as permitted under Section 107 or 108 of the 1976 U.S. Copyright Act, without the prior written permission of the publisher.

Legal Notice

This work is protected under U.S. and international copyright law. It is for personal use only and may not be distributed, sold, quoted, or paraphrased without written consent from the publisher.

Disclaimer Notice

The information in this publication is provided for educational and informational purposes only. While every effort has been made to ensure accuracy, no warranties of any kind are expressed or implied. The publisher and author make no representations regarding completeness or suitability of the material contained herein.

Readers acknowledge that neither the author nor the publisher is engaged in rendering medical, legal, financial, or professional advice. The content is based on sources believed to be reliable, but readers should consult qualified professionals before applying any techniques or practices mentioned.

By reading this work, the reader agrees that under no circumstances shall the author or publisher be liable for any loss or damages—direct or indirect—resulting from the use of the information contained within this book.

CONTENTS

INTRODUCTION

What if your bank account quietly grew while you slept, traveled the world, or spent precious moments with loved ones? Imagine waking up to more money than when you went to bed — not because of a promotion or an extra shift, but because you built smart systems that work for you around the clock. For most people, this sounds like a distant dream reserved for lottery winners or tech prodigies. Society has conditioned us to believe that wealth is earned only through relentless effort — sacrificing evenings and weekends in the name of productivity. Yet there's another way — one that doesn't depend on luck, nonstop hustle, or unrealistic promises. This book will show you how passive income can become a practical, achievable path to financial independence.

My name is Lucas Sterling, and I didn't grow up wealthy. My journey began in a small town where my parents worked multiple jobs just to make ends meet. I vividly remember the anxiety that came with every bill and the heavy belief that success was always out of reach. For years, I chased security the traditional way — working harder, taking overtime, and accepting that exhaustion was the price of survival. Then I discovered a simple truth: real freedom isn't earned by adding more hours to your day but by building smart systems that create value long after the work is done. That realization changed everything, and it's the driving force behind this book. The principles and strategies you'll find here aren't abstract theory or empty motivation — they're hard-won lessons from experience, battle-tested models, and practical tools that have helped me and many others build lasting prosperity.

Before we begin this journey, it's crucial to clarify what passive income really means — and to dispel the myths that surround it. Passive income isn't a get-rich-quick scheme or a promise of effortless wealth. The internet is full of scams claiming "overnight success" and easy riches, but let me be clear: that's not what you'll find here. True passive income is built by investing time, resources, or expertise upfront to create assets or systems that require minimal ongoing effort. Think of earning royalties from a book you wrote once or collecting rent from a well-managed property. Compare that to active income, which demands constant labor — salaries, hourly wages, or freelance work that all depend on trading your time for money. Even side hustles, while helpful, often keep your income tied to your hours. Passive income, by contrast, breaks that link. It lets you focus on scaling, automating, and optimizing your revenue streams so you can dedicate your energy to what matters most.

Never before has financial resilience been more essential. Economic instability, global uncertainty, and the rapid rise of automation and artificial intelligence are reshaping the job market at unprecedented speed. Modern work culture has left millions exhausted and disillusioned, shattering the illusion that a single paycheck guarantees stability. As traditional employment grows less secure, building a diversified income portfolio is no longer optional — it's vital. Passive income offers more than financial reward; it provides autonomy over your time, your location, and your choices. It serves as a safety net when markets fluctuate, industries evolve, or life delivers the unexpected. Most importantly, it empowers you to design a future on your own terms — whether that means traveling the world, launching a business, or simply having more time for the people you love.

If you've ever felt trapped in the endless trade of time for money, this book is for you. Maybe you dream of escaping the rigid nine-to-five, exploring new places, or supporting your loved ones without sacrificing your well-being. You may have no experience with investing or entrepreneurship — but if you have ambition and a willingness to learn, you're in the right place. Whether you're an aspiring entrepreneur eager to test ideas, a salaried employee longing for independence, a freelancer seeking stability, a digital nomad craving freedom, or a parent, student, or professional looking for a smarter way forward, you'll find both guidance and encouragement within these pages.

In the chapters ahead, you'll learn to identify and create passive income streams that match your skills, interests, and resources. We'll explore how to earn royalties from writing, music, and digital content; invest wisely in stocks, cryptocurrencies, and real estate investment trusts (REITs); generate stable rental income through strategic property management; build dropshipping and e-commerce ventures; automate YouTube channels for steady ad revenue; and develop online courses and digital products that continue to pay long after they're made. You'll also learn how to stack, scale, and diversify these income streams into a resilient portfolio — one that stands strong through economic shifts and market cycles.

This book is designed to be as practical as possible. Perfection isn't required. You don't need to master every method or pursue them all at once. Instead, choose one income stream that aligns with your strengths and situation, and take the first concrete step. If you have a specific goal, skip ahead to the chapter that resonates with you. Each section includes actionable summaries, simple checklists, and curated tools to accelerate your progress and eliminate guesswork. Every chapter ends with clear steps you can apply right away, so you're never left wondering what to do next.

Financial freedom doesn't depend on luck, privilege, or advanced technical skills. Anyone, regardless of background or education, can learn to build sustainable, diversified income streams. It simply requires structure, patience, and the courage to take action. begin. My goal is to give you the knowledge, frameworks, and confidence to design your own path, one that leads not only to wealth but also to genuine freedom and fulfillment.

Now is the time to reclaim control of your financial life. Let's build your independence, one income stream at a time.

UNLOCK YOUR FINANCIAL FREEDOM BLUEPRINT

Ready to turn your financial goals into real, actionable progress?

As a thank-you for reading this book, I've created a powerful companion resource: **The Financial Freedom Blueprint**. This exclusive, step-by-step guide helps you identify your ideal money path, plug income leaks, and make smart, aligned decisions fast. It's designed to take you from financial confusion to confidence in just a few focused steps.

What's included in this resource:

- Clarify your goals
- Streamline your expenses
- Align your spending with your values
- Start building real wealth now!

👉 **Access Your Financial Blueprint Today**
Visit: **https://content.toptierpress.com/unlock-financial-freedom**

Or scan the QR code below to get instant access!

ONE
THE FOUNDATIONS OF PASSIVE INCOME

Many people dream of earning money while they sleep, picturing a life free from the daily grind of a traditional job. The idea of passive income, money that flows in with little ongoing effort, has captured the imagination of aspiring entrepreneurs and professionals alike. Nevertheless, for many, this vision remains elusive. Despite sincere intentions and hard work, countless individuals struggle to build income streams that truly operate without constant attention. They discover themselves caught between misconceptions and reality, unsure why their efforts don't translate into lasting financial freedom.

The challenge lies not only in understanding what passive income really means but also in recognizing how it differs from the active work most are familiar with. Many attempt quick fixes or chase "easy" opportunities, only to encounter setbacks, confusion, or burnout. Success requires more than just starting; it demands patience, strategy, and a mindset shift toward long-term thinking.

This chapter explores the foundations of passive income by defining its true nature, contrasting it with active income, and revealing common pitfalls that cause many to fail. It then guides readers toward adopting the mindset needed to navigate their passive income journey effectively. By developing realistic expectations and embracing a builder's mindset, anyone can begin to lay the groundwork for sustainable, scalable income streams that contribute to genuine financial independence.

UNDERSTANDING PASSIVE INCOME: DEFINITIONS, CHARACTERISTICS, AND KEY DIFFERENCES

Passive income is the money you earn with little or no daily effort to maintain or grow it after the initial setup. Its core features include recurring revenue, minimal maintenance requirements, and the potential for scalability. Understanding these aspects is the first step to seeing why passive income attracts so much attention and why it's often misunderstood.

Recurring revenue is the backbone of genuine passive income. Instead of one-off payments, this income flows into your account repeatedly, whether you're working currently or not. For example, an author receives book royalties every time a copy sells, even years after writing it. Investors collect dividends from stocks regularly, and landlords earn rental income from tenants month after month. These streams share the common trait of persistence, once established, money keeps coming without needing to restart the process.

The minimal maintenance required is what sets passive income apart from most side hustles or jobs. You might spend time upfront creating a digital product such as an ebook or a set of templates. Once launched online, sales, delivery, and customer service can run automatically through e-commerce systems or third-party marketplaces. This frees you from daily management and repetitive tasks, allowing you to focus on new projects or simply enjoy the results.

Scalability is the key that unlocks greater financial independence through passive income. Unlike traditional work, where earnings are tied to hours worked, scalable passive income allows one piece of effort to generate returns again and again, no matter how many people purchase it. Imagine designing an online course. The upfront work is significant — writing lessons, editing videos, and building a sales page

— but once complete, it can educate dozens or even thousands of students, earning income from each one without additional labor.

Many people encounter myths about passive income that distort their expectations. Some believe it's instant and effortless — that you can set up something today and start earning tomorrow. The truth is different. All genuine passive income sources require effort, skill, or capital at the beginning. An author spends months writing a book before receiving royalties. A landlord invests time and money securing property before collecting rent.

Another common myth is that passive income is risk-free. In reality, every passive income source carries some level of risk. Book sales can fizzle out, rental properties may sit vacant or need repairs, and even dividend-paying stocks can lose value or be affected by market swings. Each opportunity demands thoughtful research, ongoing monitoring, and a willingness to adapt.

There's also confusion about what activities count as passive income. Let's clarify the differences:

Income Type	Maintenance Level	Example
True Passive	Very Low	Rental property managed by a company
Semi-Passive	Low to Moderate	Blog needing periodic content updates
Active Marketed as Passive	High	Day trading or gig work with inconsistent results

True passive income, like a rental property managed by professionals, lets your investment work with minimal input. In contrast, a blog that brings ad revenue can seem passive, but needs fresh content, updates, and marketing. Day trading, sometimes promoted as the ultimate freedom-generating strategy, is in fact highly time-consuming. It requires near-constant attention and exposes you to significant risk, making it active work rather than genuine passive income.

To grasp the distinction further, consider the time-for-money relationship:

- With active income (like freelancing), every dollar earned reflects time spent working. Miss a day, lose a day's pay.
- With passive income, your effort is concentrated at the beginning. Write a book or build a course today, and you might reap earnings automatically for years to come. An initial push combined with patience brings ongoing rewards.

For aspiring entrepreneurs and professionals, this shift means thinking in longer timelines. It can take months or even a few years before passive income streams reliably grow and start covering living expenses. Building true passive income requires dedication to creating value upfront, a willingness to learn from challenges, and the patience to see your investments pay off over time.

The journey to passive income isn't always easy, and it's not void of effort at any stage. But the advantage is clear: instead of exchanging hours for dollars indefinitely, you're building assets that can grant you greater freedom and security. Success in passive income comes down to adopting a strategic mindset, focusing on sustainable growth, and seeking opportunities that match your skills and resources. Letting go of "quick win" fantasies and embracing realistic expectations sets the foundation for genuine financial independence and a more flexible future.

THE PSYCHOLOGY OF SUCCESS: OVERCOMING PITFALLS AND SHIFTING TO A BUILDER'S MINDSET

The dream of passive income often falters at the starting line, not because earning money outside of a traditional job is impossible, but because of how people approach the journey. At the heart of most failures is impatience. Many enter the world of passive income expecting results in weeks or months, influenced by loud promises of "overnight success" from social media or online ads. When the early effort produces little or nothing, discouragement takes over. Imagine someone who launches an affiliate website, checks their earnings after only a month, and, seeing a balance of $5, decides it's not worth the hassle. This impatience leads them to abandon what could have become a steady, profitable stream.

Unrealistic expectations often feed this impatience. The idea that passive income means "no work" is widespread but dangerously misleading. Building a successful YouTube channel, for example, requires months, often years, of creating, refining, learning from feedback, and persisting through low view counts. The allure of skipping this grind is strong; so many people flit from one "hot" opportunity to another, never staying the course long enough to see real growth.

This lack of focus is another major downfall. It's easy, in today's world, to jump from dropshipping to real estate wholesaling to digital courses and back again. With every switch, valuable time and attention get diverted; instead of mastering the details of one business, people become dabblers. Resources are spread thin; you cannot properly analyze a rental property, edit a video series, and manage a Shopify store all at once. Real growth happens through deep work, not shallow dabbling.

Another stumbling block comes from within: overthinking and fear of making mistakes. Many would-be creators get stuck "perfecting" their product forever. Consider Priya, an instructional designer who spends six months refining her online course, tirelessly editing and re-recording. She reads forums, tweaks video quality, polishes slides, and second-guesses pricing but never launches. She ends up with a polished course no one ever sees. Similarly, there's David, who has studied rental property investing for years, analyzing hundreds of listings but never making an offer. Both are trapped by analysis paralysis, never turning learning into action.

Each of these barriers is surmountable. First, changing expectations is crucial. Sustainable passive income almost always begins with small steps, not grand gestures. "Small" can mean launching a minimum viable product, a seven-page ebook instead of a full masterclass, or renting out one spare room instead of buying an entire apartment complex. Small projects are less risky, easier to manage, and faster to deliver. Early wins build confidence and provide data for improvement.

Focusing on one stream at a time brings significant benefits. Concentrating on a single project makes it far easier to learn fast, iterate, and develop expertise. For instance, Mia decides to start with print-on-demand T-shirts. She creates ten basic designs, sets a goal to make her first sale within 30 days, and tracks daily traffic to her online store. Once sales become steady, she considers branching out. This sharp focus accelerates learning, keeps tasks manageable, and leads to more meaningful results.

Consistency is essential, but it needs to be defined by practical, measurable actions. Instead of vague commitments, successful builders set clear milestones: uploading one new YouTube video per week, running five product ads daily, or submitting three new real estate offers per month. These micro-goals pile up over time. Luca, who saw no rental income for his first six months, remained committed to analyzing five properties a week and submitting two offers each month. It took nine months to close his first deal, but by then, his habits and skills were solidified.

Success in passive income also comes from thinking like a builder or owner, not just a consumer. The consumer mentality seeks entertainment, easy answers, and quick rewards. Builders investigate how to solve problems and create value, even when the initial payoff is invisible. This shift can be practiced by making tiny decisions: writing instead of scrolling social media, following up with leads instead of waiting for them, or choosing to learn a new skill with direct application. Over time, this mindset becomes second nature.

Linking passive income goals to personal values keeps motivation strong through setbacks. Melissa, a busy parent, connects her pursuit of rental income to her desire for flexible family time. When obstacles arise, she remembers her deeper purpose, which fuels her discipline to keep going when progress feels slow. Powerful passive income efforts are always grounded in clear, personal reasons that outlast temporary frustrations.

Success is not about perfect timing or flawless execution but about starting small, staying focused, acting consistently, and building with intention.

Now that we have clarified what passive income truly entails, how it differs from active income, and the common obstacles that hinder success, readers will be equipped to approach this journey with a realistic and patient mindset. Building sustainable passive income requires focused effort, consistent action, and a willingness to learn and adapt over time. By setting clear goals, concentrating on one opportunity at a time, and aligning efforts with personal values, aspiring entrepreneurs can overcome challenges and gradually create reliable income streams that provide greater financial freedom. Embracing this builder's mindset positions you not just to earn money passively but to build lasting assets that support long-term independence and flexibility beyond the traditional work model.

TWO
SETTING YOUR FINANCIAL FREEDOM GOAL

Imagine waking each day without the pressure of a rigid schedule or without financial stress dictating your choices. For some, this freedom means pursuing passions long set aside; for others, it represents security and flexibility to spend time with family or explore new ventures. Yet despite these varied visions, many aspiring entrepreneurs and professionals struggle to define what true financial independence looks like for themselves. Without a clear target, the path to sustained income beyond the traditional job can feel uncertain and overwhelming.

This chapter guides you in discovering your unique vision of financial freedom by reflecting on what matters most in your life. It will help you calculate a personalized "freedom number", the monthly amount needed to support your ideal lifestyle and develop practical methods to track your progress. By connecting your mindset with measurable financial goals, you create a foundation that supports consistent growth in multiple income streams. Through building effective budgeting habits and sustaining motivation, you prepare yourself not just to dream about financial independence but to take deliberate, focused steps toward achieving it.

CLARIFYING YOUR PERSONAL FINANCIAL FREEDOM AND CALCULATING YOUR FREEDOM NUMBER

Imagine one person's financial freedom means stepping away from boardrooms to start a rescue center for stray animals. For someone else, it might mean never feeling rushed in the morning, sipping homemade coffee on their balcony with loved ones nearby. Each person's blueprint feels different, because freedom doesn't have a single form. Consider Maria, who led major corporate teams for years but felt her real purpose was launching a nonprofit focused on literacy. Her freedom looks like early meetings with passionate volunteers and afternoons organizing book drives, with more time for her teenage children at home. In another scenario, Sam teaches high school science but dreams of running an online tutoring business from anywhere in the world. He pictures exploring new countries every few months, his laptop his only office. Then there's Jasmine and David, raising two kids in a lively suburb; they see financial independence as stress-free college funds, family trips to national parks, and enough flexibility for David to transition from a demanding tech job into freelance consulting.

These stories show that financial independence isn't a fixed destination; it's about creating a life shaped by your values, preferences, and dreams. Instead of keeping up with external expectations, you define what truly matters.

A powerful way to discover your personal vision is through a guided visualization exercise. Choose a quiet spot. Sit, close your eyes, and breathe deeply. Imagine your best day after you've achieved financial freedom. What time do you wake up? Who are you with? Where do you live? How do you spend your time throughout the day, from your morning coffee to your evening relaxation? Do you work on creative projects, travel, or focus on relationships? Notice the sounds, textures, colors, and the overall mood of your ideal day. Ask yourself: What activities fill you with purpose? Which moments bring you peace or excitement? What do you never want to go back to? Next, reflect on the feelings this ideal day evokes. Write down words that describe your mood: calm, joyful, energized, relieved. Then consider what these insights suggest about your real priorities. List three or four realizations or unexpected desires that stand out. Finally, review your notes and record the key details in a notebook or digital document. They're your personal North Star for shaping your freedom plan.

Turning vision into tangible action starts with knowing exactly what you need each month to make it real: a concrete "freedom number." Here's how to pinpoint yours, step by step.

1. Make a table of all your fixed monthly expenses. These might include rent or mortgage, utilities, insurance, car payments, cell phone bills, and healthcare premiums.
2. List variable costs — groceries, transportation, dining out, entertainment, hobbies, clothing, and personal care.
3. Add line items for the upgrades you'd love — occasional weekend trips, new tech gear, fitness classes, more shows or concerts, or that upgraded streaming bundle.
4. Consider contributions to savings, retirement, or investment accounts for long-term security.
5. Finally, add a 20% buffer to protect your lifestyle if emergencies or one-off expenses pop up.

Example Table: Freedom Number Calculation

Category	Minimalist Nomad	Suburban Family	Urban Professional
Housing/utilities	$1,400	$2,800	$3,500
Food	$400	$1,200	$1,100
Transportation	$200	$800	$500
Insurance/healthcare	$250	$750	$600
Lifestyle/upgrades	$400	$1,000	$2,200
Savings/investing	$200	$750	$1,000
Entertainment	$150	$400	$850
Education/other	•	$550	$550
20% Security buffer	$600	$1,300	$2,000
Total/Month	**$3,000**	**$8,000**	**$12,000**

For Jamie, the minimalist nomad, home is a series of short-term rentals across Southeast Asia. Fixed costs include $900 for accommodation, $500 for food, and modest insurance premiums. Jamie values flexibility and adventure over luxury. Savings and upgrade buckets allow for monthly treks and online learning. Their freedom number, including the buffer, totals $3,000.

The Carters, living in a suburban neighborhood, need consistency for their kids' schooling and activities. Their $2,500 mortgage supports a comfortable home base. Utilities and groceries run higher, plus sports and music for the children. They want vacations and bigger family outings. Aiming for $8,000 monthly gives them confidence to invest in their future.

Priya, the urban professional, lives in a downtown condo, walking to a favorite bistro on weekends. She enjoys theater, fitness studios, and robust savings for early retirement. High housing costs, elevated utility bills, health and wellness extras, and creative pursuits make her monthly freedom number $12,000 — with a comfortable buffer for surprises.

Your freedom number comes from these choices — what you value, where you thrive, and how you wish to grow. It isn't just covering needs; it should leave space for security, upgrades, and future plans. Remember, passive income from investments or ventures will help reach this target, but for now, focus on defining what that target is. There are no wrong answers — only the answer that lines up with your vision.

BUILDING TRACKING HABITS, BUDGETING EFFECTIVELY, AND SUSTAINING MOTIVATION

Creating a system for tracking your finances builds a solid structure for reaching your passive income goals. By maintaining clear records, you gain financial clarity that leads to better decisions — the kind that help you spot opportunities and avoid costly mistakes. When your ultimate goal is your freedom number, each tracked dollar works as a stepping stone toward that exact target.

Manual spreadsheet tracking offers a simple, accessible method to take control of your finances. This approach uses a basic spreadsheet to log every income source and expense. Most people begin by listing all inflows and outflows on a weekly or monthly basis. To implement this, set up columns for date, category, amount, and notes. Each time you spend or earn, record the transaction right away. For a side hustler, this could mean entering every purchase tied to startup supplies, while a professional might note dividend payments or stock sales. An entrepreneur juggling multiple projects can create a tab for each income stream to isolate trends. The main pitfalls with spreadsheets involve missing small purchases, getting behind on updates, or neglecting to categorize entries accurately. If you find yourself making decisions with up-to-date information, detecting overspending early, and feeling confident about your trajectory, your manual tracking is working.

Basic budgeting apps offer an intermediate level of systemization. These programs automate much of the data entry by syncing with your bank accounts and credit cards. After setup, you allocate transactions into categories and assess spending against custom budgets. Side hustlers benefit from separating business and personal flows in the app for tax preparation. Professionals tracking investment returns can set notifications for incoming dividends or changes in portfolio value. Entrepreneurs see cash flow for several ventures in one dashboard. Implementation involves downloading an app, securely connecting accounts, and categorizing at least weekly to avoid errors. Some users fall into the trap of ignoring app notifications, leading to blind spots, or relying too much on automatic categorization, which can mislabel purchases. When your app shows accurate balances, categorization matches your goals, and your freedom number's gap narrows month-to-month, your tracking is on target.

Comprehensive financial platforms represent the advanced method. These solutions integrate banking, investments, budgeting, and even tax planning in one interface. After you onboard all accounts — checking, savings, brokerage, and any business holdings — the software generates detailed reports and forecasts. A side hustler uses platform analytics to track profitability, factoring in both expenses and varied income streams. A professional monitors shifting asset allocations, dividend yield, and tax-loss harvesting. The multi-venture entrepreneur benefits from consolidated reporting on personal, business, and passive income streams. Implementing these tools involves regular review sessions, setting up custom reports, and using alerts for key events, such as dips below your target investment rate. The biggest mistakes with platforms include setup overload, ignoring data analysis, or failing to act on insights. If you consistently receive actionable recommendations, see progress toward your freedom number in your dashboards, and notice fewer surprises in your finances, your system is paying off.

Use the 70/20/10 budgeting framework to build a realistic and robust financial foundation. Assign 70% of your monthly after-tax income to living expenses, 20% to investments, and 10% to savings. This arrangement ensures living costs remain sustainable while you reserve a full fifth of your income for building passive assets. Saving 10% creates a buffer against emergencies or missed income. For example, if your current expense tracking shows $3,000 per month, the framework suggests no more than $2,100 for living costs, $600 for investments, and $300 directed strictly to savings. By sticking to this breakdown, you architect your finances specifically for long-term freedom.

For a practical step, dedicate a week to logging every expense. Review receipts and bank statements to classify spending as needs or wants, such as housing and groceries versus streaming subscriptions and takeout. Calculate your current percentage of income going to investments. Compare your habits to the 70/20/10 framework by constructing a simple table:

Category	Current Allocation	Framework Target	Difference
Living Expenses	$2,500 (83%)	$2,100 (70%)	+$400
Investments	$350 (12%)	$600 (20%)	-$250
Savings	$150 (5%)	$300 (10%)	-$150

Identify excesses in living costs or areas where investment contributions fall short. Reallocate funds accordingly to optimize progress.

Motivation grows when you connect everyday habits to visible progress. Develop a simple monitoring system where you track milestones like meeting your monthly passive income goal, hitting a new investment diversification benchmark, reducing monthly discretionary expenses, and increasing your freedom number buffer. Healthy progress might look like achieving a $100 increase in monthly passive income or lowering grocery bills by $50 through meal planning. Avoid demotivating comparisons such as measuring your pace against online personalities.

Anchor your system with habits that make tracking sustainable: schedule a weekly review of accounts, adapt goals during a monthly check-in, celebrate quarterly achievements such as your first $1,000 in passive income, and revisit your overall strategy each year. This structure keeps your financial foundation strong and your eyes focused on the next stage — putting your tracking to work in building real, recurring passive income.

Having now defined your unique vision of financial freedom, calculated your personalized freedom number, and established a practical framework for tracking and budgeting, you are equipped to take intentional steps toward your goals. With clarity on what matters most to you and a realistic action plan rooted in disciplined habits, you can confidently build and grow multiple streams of passive income. Embracing this tailored approach empowers you to move beyond uncertainty, steadily closing the gap between your current reality and the life you envision. As you implement these strategies, your focus will sharpen, motivation will strengthen, and each small milestone will bring you closer to lasting financial independence and the freedom to live on your own terms.

THREE
EARNING FROM ROYALTIES AND INTELLECTUAL PROPERTY

Have you ever wondered how some creators manage to earn money long after their work is finished? Imagine writing a book, composing music, or creating art once and then receiving payments on that effort for months or even years without additional active work. This idea of generating income from intellectual property — spreading your creative output across different formats and platforms — is something many aspire to but few fully understand.

Turning creativity, knowledge, or expertise into a steady stream of royalties offers a way to build financial independence beyond the usual paycheck-to-paycheck cycle. It requires not only producing quality content but also knowing how to leverage publishing tools, distribution channels, and legal protections. The potential lies in creating assets that continue to earn through multiple formats like ebooks, audiobooks, translations, and prints, which can expand reach and diversify earnings over time. In this chapter, we will examine the foundations of royalty income and intellectual property, exploring how to transform your work into scalable, recurring revenue sources while safeguarding your rights.

MONETIZING BOOKS, MUSIC, PHOTOGRAPHY, AND ART

Aspiring authors and creators leverage royalty-based income streams by publishing digital books, print-on-demand paperbacks, and audiobooks on major platforms. Amazon Kindle Direct Publishing (KDP) leads the self-publishing landscape for ebooks and paperbacks, providing broad market access and transparent royalty models. KDP allows authors to upload manuscripts in formats like DOCX or PDF through a clear, step-by-step dashboard. The interface displays fields for book title, author name, description, categories, and keywords. When uploading a manuscript, KDP's preview tool reveals how the finished ebook or paperback will appear on Kindle devices and in print. The royalty structure for ebooks is straightforward: authors set list prices between $2.99 and $9.99 to access a 70% royalty rate (minus a small delivery fee) in eligible regions. For paperbacks, royalties are set at 60% of the list price minus printing costs, typically around $2.15 for a standard black-and-white US print.

In contrast, audiobooks are distributed via Audible ACX and Findaway Voices. Audiobook production can require more upfront investment but offers unique income channels. ACX, Audible's own platform, enables authors to recruit narrators, pay per finished hour, or split royalties. ACX pays 40% royalties for exclusive distribution to Audible, Amazon, and iTunes, or 25% for non-exclusive distribution. Findaway Voices provides access to more retailers but offers a flat 45% royalty from sales, with broader reach. Both platforms require completed audio files, standardized opening/closing credits, a retail sample, and adherence to quality requirements such as specific bit rates and RMS levels.

Successful authors who publish across these formats illustrate the potential of self-publishing. For example, Mark Dawson, a thriller novelist, consistently reports six-figure annual royalties from his KDP titles, amplified by effective email marketing and advertising. Rachel Morgan, a young adult author, gained traction with a focused fantasy niche, reporting royalties of $7,000–$10,000 per month from combined ebook, paperback, and audiobook sales. Earnings vary; a single well-performing ebook series can generate $20,000–$100,000 per year, while a top-selling audiobook can add another $5,000–$50,000, provided that content reaches a sizable audience and maintains high review scores.

Choosing content with long-term earning potential starts with researching evergreen topics and niche opportunities. Use Amazon's bestseller charts, keyword research tools like Publisher Rocket, and competitor analysis to identify categories with steady demand and low-to-moderate competition. Search for topics with consistent ranks in the Kindle Store's top 1,000 or those with thousands of existing reviews but little recent release activity. To validate a topic, estimate monthly sales using the Amazon Best Sellers Rank (BSR) to earnings calculators; for example, a title ranked #5,000 in Kindle may sell 200–300 copies per month.

Efficient content creation combines structured writing, high editing standards, and production support. Many successful authors outsource parts of the process. Ghostwriters charge $0.03–$0.15 per word based on experience and genre, while editors cost $300–$1,200 per manuscript depending on length and depth of service (developmental vs. copy editing). Professional cover designers range from $50 to $300, and AI-assisted tools like Grammarly, ProWritingAid, and Sudowrite streamline grammar, tone, and style checks. Budgeting $1,000–$2,500 for full production and marketing is typical for first-time publishers seeking strong results.

Quality control is essential. KDP and ACX provide precise formatting requirements: EPUB for ebooks, print-ready PDFs for paperbacks, and structured WAV or MP3 files for audiobooks. All platforms demand clearly defined metadata — titles, subtitles, categories, keywords — that maximize discoverability. Metadata optimization includes focusing on genre keywords, search intent, and accurate category selection. Writing compelling and concise book descriptions directly shapes conversion rates.

Pricing strategies combine competitive list pricing, limited-time promotions, and strategic series bundling. Many authors experiment with Amazon's Kindle Countdown Deals or free promotions to gather early reviews and boost initial visibility. Audiobooks, with price points ranging from $9.99 to $29.99, include options like Audible's credit and subscription systems, which can affect payout consistency.

Marketing fundamentals revolve around building email lists, reader engagement, and leveraging Amazon Ads or BookBub campaigns to drive traffic. Tracking sales, download data, and royalty statements in real-time dashboards provides immediate insights for adjusting strategies. Comparing options, KDP offers higher ebook royalties and visibility, while ACX/Findaway capture audio listeners seeking premium content.

Initial publishing might take 1–3 months, depending on content complexity and service availability. Upfront costs represent a risk, but careful niche selection, consistent quality, and attentive marketing lower the chance of unprofitability. Once content is launched, royalties provide truly passive income. Content translated into new languages and repurposed across ebook, print, and audio formats amplifies reach and diversifies revenue even further.

EXPANDING REVENUE STREAMS AND PROTECTING YOUR WORK

When a creator understands the power of format multiplication, a single content asset can produce steady, diversified revenue streams. For example, consider a self-published entrepreneur who launched a practical business guide. Initial earnings came from ebook and paperback sales via Amazon KDP and IngramSpark, generating $450 monthly — 70% from ebook, 30% paperback. In the second month, they produced an audiobook using ACX, investing $300 in narration, and released across Audible, Apple Books, and Google Play. Audiobook sales contributed an additional $320 monthly, with Audible representing 80% of those royalties. By month four, the book was translated into Spanish and German (each translation averaging $700 and three weeks to complete), distributed via Draft2Digital and Kobo Writing Life, and promoted through region-specific Amazon ads and Spanish-language podcast sponsorships. These editions averaged $180 monthly per translated market, bringing total monthly income above $1,000 and consistently growing.

Creators follow a process built on strategic planning and platform knowledge. After establishing the original format, expand reach by offering audiobook versions — either by narrating personally or through professional talent. Major platforms, such as ACX, offer 40% royalty for exclusive distribution and 25% for non-exclusive. Extend further with translations using reputable freelancers via Reedsy or Babelcube. Royalties on Babelcube, for instance, begin at 30%, rising to 85% after $2,000 in sales. Market these adaptations through targeted ads, coordinated launch campaigns, and territory-focused partnerships. This multi-format approach not only multiplies income but also strengthens brand presence across diverse segments.

Format Multiplication Planning

Take these direct steps:

- Write your primary content asset (e.g., an English-language small business starter guide)
- Identify three format transformations:
  a. Audiobook version ($300 narration cost, projected monthly sales: $250)
  b. The Spanish ebook and print-on-demand (POD) release will incur a translation cost of $700, with projected monthly sales estimated at $120.
  c. The German audiobook has a translation and narration cost of $900, with projected monthly sales of $130.

- Calculate potential revenue: (Ebook $400) + (Audiobook $250) + (Spanish $120) + (German $130) = $900/mo
- Create a 6-month timeline:
  - Month 1: Ebook/Paperback launch
  - Month 2: Audiobook production and release
  - Month 3–4: Spanish translation and publication
  - Month 5: Spanish audiobook or next language expansion
  - Month 6: German publication and marketing

This plan transforms a single content asset into a multi-stream earning engine within 180 days.

Legal Protections in Format Expansion

Every format multiplied must be protected by clear, proactive legal actions. Copyright registration in your primary jurisdiction provides legal proof and damages eligibility in infringement claims. In the US, you can register a single work within 90 days of its publication on copyright.gov for $65 through electronic filing. Internationally, rely on the Berne Convention's automatic protection, but always verify local requirements in new markets.

Clear contracts are essential when commissioning translations, audiobook productions, or designer collaborations. A strong contract details work-for-hire status (if applicable), payment, delivery deadlines, rights assignment, and territory coverage. Determine usage rights at the start — do you want exclusive or non-exclusive rights? Platforms such as ACX require contractual confirmation of distribution rights and territory specifics. When expanding into print, assign your ISBN through Bowker ($125 for a block of 10 ISBNs in the US), and file for copyright registration.

Legal Protection Framework

Apply these direct steps:

- File copyright registration at copyright.gov within 90 days; retain the completion certificate.
- Draw up contracts listing rights, deliverables, scope, and payment; review for completeness.
- Decide on licensing and usage rights per format: assign exclusive rights for audiobooks or translations if higher royalties are offered.
- Check each platform's legal requirements; on Spotify or Apple Music, music requires mechanical and performance rights clearance (managed via Harry Fox Agency or BMI, $75 setup and variable royalty rates). For art, clarify licensing terms —

e.g., one-time fee vs. royalty percentage, duration, and territories.

- For books: obtain ISBN, file copyright, attach clear contracts with collaborators.
- For music: register with PRO (ASCAP, BMI), obtain mechanical licenses, maintain explicit distributor contracts.
- For visual art: draft licensing agreements, state usage restrictions, document any exclusive rights granted.

IP Protection Audit

Follow this practical implementation:

- List all current IP assets and their legal registration status.
- Spot any assets without copyright registration, lack of contracts, or unclear ownership.
- Take action: register copyrights online today, draft missing contracts, and renegotiate any ambiguous terms.
- Organize documentation: certificates, executed contracts, platform receipts, and email confirmations in digital files.

One entrepreneur, starting with a single small business guide, earned $450/mo from sales. Format expansion (audiobook, Spanish/German editions) doubled monthly revenue in six months. Copyright filing within three weeks of launch deterred pirated online editions. Each contract for translation assigned exclusive language rights, with automated royalty splits managed via Babelcube and ACX. ISBN assignment for every print edition ensured global tracking and retail eligibility.

This section empowers creators to multiply their intellectual property's income while securing their future earnings. The upcoming downloadable "IP Income Starter Kit" checklist gives you every tool to put these strategies into action.

Now that you understand how to harness the power of royalty-based income and intellectual property, you can begin transforming your knowledge, creativity, or expertise into scalable and recurring revenue streams. By strategically creating content across multiple formats; e-books, audiobooks, translations, and print editions, and securing your rights through proper legal protections, you set the foundation for sustainable passive income that grows over time. With careful planning, quality production, and targeted marketing, you can multiply your earnings, expand your reach globally, and build a diversified portfolio that moves you closer to financial independence. Embracing these methods empowers you to break free from traditional income limitations and confidently shape a future defined by ongoing, automated returns on your intellectual investments.

FOUR
BUILDING WEALTH THROUGH STOCKS AND DIVIDENDS

Have you ever wondered how some people manage to create a steady flow of income without having to clock in every day? Many dream of building financial security that works quietly in the background, supporting their goals without constant effort or expertise. Yet for those unfamiliar with investing, especially the complexities of the stock market, this idea can feel overwhelming or out of reach.

The world of stocks often seems exclusive to experts or wealthy individuals, and the idea of earning money just by owning shares seems unreal. Questions arise: How do dividends actually work? Can someone without a finance background really build wealth through stocks? And what steps can turn this passive income into a reliable source over time? This chapter will guide you through understanding dividend investing and how it can serve as a cornerstone in creating a sustainable income portfolio. With clear explanations and practical insights, it aims to empower you to navigate the stock market confidently and develop a long-term strategy for growing your wealth steadily and securely.

FOUNDATIONS OF DIVIDEND INVESTING AND BUILDING A MONTHLY INCOME PORTFOLIO

Dividend investing offers a way for individuals to build wealth by receiving a share of company profits as cash payments. These payments, known as dividends, are typically paid quarterly, but some companies may distribute them monthly or annually. When you own stock in a company that pays dividends, you receive regular deposits of money, usually credited directly to your brokerage account. Companies known for steady dividends include giants like Coca-Cola, Johnson & Johnson, and Procter & Gamble. By sharing excess profits with shareholders, these businesses signal financial health and a long-term commitment to returning value.

Dividends are not guaranteed, but many established companies aim to maintain or raise their payouts year after year. For example, if you own 100 shares of a company that pays $0.50 per share each quarter, you receive $50 every three months simply for holding your shares. This predictable income stream is attractive to investors seeking stability, such as retirees or those planning for long-term goals. A company's dividend yield, expressed as a percentage, tells you how much annual income you can expect in relation to the stock's current price. For instance, if a stock trades at $50 and pays a $2 annual dividend, its yield is 4%.

An effective way to maximize the power of dividends is through DRIPs, or Dividend Reinvestment Plans. A DRIP automatically uses the cash dividends you receive to purchase more shares of the company instead of depositing the payment in your account. This reinvestment takes place every dividend cycle, harnessing the benefit of compound growth. Compounding means you earn dividends on your original investment as well as previous dividends that have been reinvested, creating a snowball effect over time.

Consider a straightforward example. Imagine investing $1,000 in a company with a 4% annual dividend yield. Without a DRIP, you would receive $40 per year in cash. By enrolling in a DRIP, those $40 buy more shares, which in turn generate further dividends. If the stock price and dividend yield remain constant, the following year you would own $1,040 worth of stock, and your dividend would rise to $41.60. Over multiple years, this compounding accelerates growth — after 10 years, your original $1,000 could grow to approximately $1,480, excluding stock price changes. If the company increases its dividend or the stock appreciates, growth is even more significant.

Dividend investing provides three key advantages. First, it delivers predictable income. Most companies pay on set schedules — quarterly payments are common, meaning you receive income every three months. Some real estate investment trusts (REITs) and special funds may pay monthly. Second, there's long-term growth potential. Many renowned companies, known as "dividend aristocrats," have raised dividends every year for decades. For example, Johnson & Johnson and Coca-Cola have increased dividends annually for over 50 years, rewarding long-term shareholders with rising payouts even during market downturns. Third, dividend investing is appealing for its low-maintenance nature. Once you select reliable dividend payers and enroll in a DRIP, your investment grows automatically with very little ongoing management. You do not need to monitor prices or trade frequently.

Getting started with dividend investing does not require large sums of money. Many brokerage platforms now allow you to buy partial shares with as little as $1. Several offer commission-free trading, making it easy for beginners to start small and grow over time. Here is a comparison of three popular platforms:

Platform	Minimum Investment	Dividends Auto-Reinvestment	User Experience	Unique Feature
Robinhood	$1	Yes (automated)	Simple, fast signup	User-friendly mobile interface
M1 Finance	$10	Yes (customizable pies)	Streamlined, goal-based	Automated portfolio rebalancing
eToro	$10	Yes (with fractional shares)	Social investing tools	CopyTrader (mimic top investors)

Through these platforms, you can research dividend-paying stocks, open a brokerage account, and activate DRIP or reinvestment features on your dashboard. To calculate potential returns, multiply the number of shares owned by the dividend per share for total annual income, or use the dividend yield to estimate returns on your investment. For instance, owning 50 shares of a company that pays $1 per share yearly brings $50 in annual dividends. To estimate compounded growth with DRIP, online calculators can help you factor in reinvested earnings and potential dividend increases.

Dividend investors have the flexibility to choose between individual stocks, such as blue-chip companies, and index funds or ETFs that bundle many dividend-paying stocks together. Index funds, especially those focused on dividends, offer built-in diversification, ease of management, and smoother performance. Individual stocks, on the other hand, allow targeted exposure but require more research and monitoring.

Whether you prefer a set-and-forget approach or want to handpick stocks, you can start building income-generating portfolios with confidence and clarity by understanding these basics and using beginner-friendly tools.

OPTIMIZING TAXES, REINVESTMENT STRATEGIES, AND PRACTICAL TOOLS FOR DIVIDEND INVESTORS

Qualified dividends usually come from shares of large, established companies such as Microsoft (MSFT) or Johnson & Johnson (JNJ). These dividends meet IRS criteria and are taxed at the lower long-term capital gains rates — 0%, 15%, or 20% depending on your income. By contrast, ordinary dividends may arise from real estate investment trusts (REITs), like Realty Income (O), or master limited partnerships (MLPs). These are taxed as regular income, potentially up to 37%. For instance, if you earn $1,000 in qualified dividends from Coca-Cola (KO) and fall into the 15% capital gains bracket, you owe $150 in taxes. An equal $1,000 from a REIT, taxed at your 24% income rate, results in a $240 tax bill. The distinction can significantly affect your after-tax returns.

Dividend Source	Tax Category	Example Stock	Tax Rate (Mid Bracket)	Tax Owed ($1,000)
MSFT, KO	Qualified Dividend	MSFT, KO	15%	$150
Realty Income (O)	Ordinary Dividend	REIT	24%	$240

Common pitfalls involve overloading a taxable brokerage account with high-yielding ordinary dividend stocks, leading to tax bills that erode real returns. Investors often don't consider the asset type's tax impact — holding REITs in a taxable account, for example, rather than inside a tax-sheltered IRA.

To implement an efficient structure:

- First, review each holding's dividend qualities.
- Place qualified dividend stocks in taxable accounts, but prioritize REITs or MLPs for Traditional or Roth IRAs.
- Rebalance annually to keep tax efficiency aligned with your investment goals.

Selecting the optimal account is often just as crucial as picking the right stock. In a traditional IRA or 401(k), dividends grow tax-deferred; taxes are paid on withdrawal, typically at a lower bracket in retirement. Roth IRAs offer tax-free growth and withdrawal. Taxable accounts, however, tax dividends each year — unless qualified and at a lower rate.

Account Type	Dividend Handling	Example Use Case
Traditional IRA	Tax deferred until withdrawal	Near-retiree lowering taxable income over time
Roth IRA	Tax-free growth and withdrawal	Early-career investor optimizing for long-term compound return
Taxable Account	Dividends taxed annually, at bracket rate	High-income individual with maxed-out retirement accounts

Mathematically, investing $10,000 in dividend stocks with a 4% qualified yield in a taxable account, taxed at 15%, grows to about $14,949 after 10 years. The same investment in a Roth IRA grows to $14,802 (similar, since taxes are avoided entirely). With ordinary dividends taxed at 24% over the same period, the taxable account reaches only about $14,332, showing the real impact of tax treatment over time.

For reinvestment, assessment criteria include:

- Your stage of life (accumulation vs. income)
- Immediate cash needs
- Growth vs. income priorities

Decision points:

- If you're early in your career, reinvesting dividends can maximize compounding.

- Approaching retirement, you may begin diverting dividends to cash for expenses.
- If you rely on investments for living expenses, regular dividend payouts make sense.

Implementation steps involve setting your brokerage for automatic dividend reinvestment (DRIP) or cash payout. Monitoring metrics include dividend yield growth, cash flow consistency, and total portfolio return.

For example, a 35-year-old reinvesting $2,000 in annual dividends at 4% sees that amount grow to about $29,601 in 30 years (with compounding). Taking dividends in cash yields just $60,000 collected over the period — showing the compounding's dramatic effect.

International investing adds a new layer of consideration. Countries like the U.K. often withhold 0-15% for U.S. investors; Canada withholds 15% with tax treaty benefits, while Switzerland withholds 35%, reduced to 15% via treaty. These rates can sometimes be reclaimed or minimized through proper paperwork (IRS Form W-8BEN for U.S. investors). Changes in currency can result in gains or losses, and broker fees for currency conversions should receive special attention. To avoid double taxation, use brokers that automatically apply tax treaty benefits and maintain clear records for foreign tax credits.

Practical tools are essential:

- Portfolio Tracker: Sharesight, Morningstar Portfolio Manager
- Tax Estimator: TurboTax TaxCaster, IRS Withholding Estimator
- Dividend Alert: Seeking Alpha, Simply Safe Dividends
- Account Aggregator: Personal Capital, Mint

Tool Type	Example	Main Function
Portfolio Tracker	Sharesight	Tracks portfolios, calculates returns, and income
Tax Calculation	TurboTax	Estimate the tax owed on dividends.
Dividend Alert	Seeking Alpha	Notifies of payouts/dividend changes
Aggregator	Personal Capital	Centralizes all financial accounts

A practical action plan for implementation:

1. Open the necessary accounts (Roth IRA, Traditional IRA, or brokerage).
2. Research and select your first stock, focusing on tax treatment and diversification.
3. Gather and store dividend records, 1099-DIV forms, and tax identification documentation.
4. Set up your portfolio monitor — choose a tracker, tax tool, and dividend alert system.

For your exercise:

- Add up last year's dividend income, classify it by type, and calculate hypothetical tax owed using current brackets.
- Choose accounts for each holding, weighing tax treatment and personal needs.
- Decide if you will automatically reinvest or take cash from each holding, justifying the choice based on your objectives.
- Establish recurring monthly or quarterly reviews using your chosen tracker and alert system.

Finally, use the downloadable Monthly Dividend Planner. This spreadsheet, integrated with your trackers, helps you plan for tax payments, schedules not-yet-received dividends, and provides a clear record for annual reporting. It ties together tax optimization, account selection, reinvestment, and monitoring — helping you maximize after-tax growth and maintain a steady dividend income stream.

Now that we understand the fundamentals of dividend investing and how to build a sustainable, long-term income portfolio — even without a financial background — we can confidently begin crafting our path to financial independence through the stock market. By selecting reliable dividend-paying stocks, leveraging reinvestment strategies such as DRIPs, and optimizing tax-efficient account choices, investors can generate predictable cash flow while harnessing the power of compounding growth over time. Equipped with practical tools and knowledge, aspiring entrepreneurs and professionals alike are well-positioned to take actionable steps toward creating diversified passive income streams that support lasting wealth and greater freedom beyond traditional employment.

FIVE
CRYPTOCURRENCY AND BLOCKCHAIN INCOME

Have you ever wondered how some people manage to earn money from cryptocurrency without constantly buying and selling? The world of digital assets is often seen as confusing and risky, especially for those new to blockchain technology. Questions about where income can come from, how much effort it takes, and what dangers might lie ahead often leave beginners unsure about taking the first step.

This chapter will explore various ways to generate passive income using cryptocurrencies. It will explain concepts like staking, yield farming, airdrops, and NFTs, showing how each method works and what you need to participate. At the same time, it will highlight important risks, such as market volatility and common scams, so you can approach opportunities with caution and confidence. By gaining a clear understanding of these options, you will be better prepared to responsibly build income streams within the blockchain ecosystem.

EARNING METHODS AND OPPORTUNITIES: STAKING, YIELD FARMING, AIRDROPS, AND NFTS

Staking allows investors to earn rewards by actively participating in the validation of blockchain transactions. On proof-of-stake networks, such as Ethereum and Cardano, users "stake" or lock up their tokens as collateral in order to validate transactions, maintain network security, and earn incentives. Ethereum requires a minimum of 32 ETH to run a solo validator node directly, with returns averaging 4–5% annually. However, pooled staking solutions like those offered by Lido or Rocket Pool permit participation with smaller amounts, as low as 0.01 ETH, while pooling assets with others. Cardano's staking is accessible through native wallets like Daedalus or Yoroi, with no strict minimum and annual rewards of approximately 4–6%. A typical staking process begins by installing the respective cryptocurrency's wallet, transferring tokens, selecting a staking pool, and delegating assets directly through the user-friendly interface. Most platforms clearly display available pools, expected yield, and fees. Beginners benefit from built-in tutorials, simple pool selection, and robust customer support. The main technical requirements include a secure wallet, a reliable internet connection, and basic familiarity with wallet operations. Staked tokens usually remain locked, meaning withdrawal is either restricted or possible only after a cooldown period.

Yield farming involves supplying digital assets to decentralized finance (DeFi) protocols in return for a share of the transaction fees or interest generated. Popular platforms such as Uniswap and Aave have streamlined tools for both liquidity provision and lending. On Uniswap, users deposit pairs of cryptocurrencies into "liquidity pools," enabling decentralized trading and earning a percentage of trading fees — typically around 0.3% of every trade proportional to their share of the pool. Aave enables users to lend assets directly, with interest rates for stablecoins like USDC or DAI often ranging from 3% to 8% APY depending on market conditions. Accessing these platforms requires connecting a Web3 wallet, such as MetaMask, to the protocol, choosing the asset or liquidity pool, and confirming the smart contract transaction. Uniswap's interface displays current liquidity, pool share, and estimated returns, while Aave provides clear APR metrics and risk scores for each asset. Minimum deposits range from a few dollars' worth of tokens on Uniswap to slightly higher for more niche assets. Most platforms operate via web browsers with straightforward dashboards, guides for deposit/withdrawal, and

24/7 digital support. The main time commitment comes from monitoring rewards, rebalancing positions, and adjusting to changing yield rates.

Airdrops serve as promotional rewards distributed by projects to active community members or early supporters. They help bootstrap user adoption and create incentives for engagement before or during a token launch. Historic examples include Uniswap's 2020 airdrop of 400 UNI tokens — worth around $3,000 at launch — to anyone who had used the platform before a certain date. Another well-known event is the dYdX airdrop, which distributed thousands of dollars' worth of tokens to traders and liquidity providers based on past usage. To qualify for airdrops, users must typically meet criteria such as holding specific assets, completing tasks, or participating in on-chain governance. Reliable platforms for tracking upcoming airdrops include CoinMarketCap's Airdrop calendar and Airdrops.io. Verifying an airdrop's authenticity requires checking official project channels, reviewing announcement details on Twitter or Discord, and avoiding requests for private keys or additional funds.

NFTs (non-fungible tokens) offer passive income opportunities beyond simple buying and selling. Creators can encode royalties, often set at 5–10%, directly into smart contracts, ensuring they automatically receive a percentage of future resale prices. On OpenSea, artists like Beeple and musicians such as 3LAU have fetched millions while earning continuous royalties from every subsequent sale. Other successful NFT projects include Decentraland (digital land), Bored Ape Yacht Club (collectibles), and Foundation (artwork). To mint and list NFTs, users create a digital wallet, connect it to a major platform (e.g., OpenSea or Rarible), and upload their digital asset. The interface guides the user through filling metadata fields, setting royalties, and paying a one-time transaction fee, called "gas." Most platforms support beginner-friendly workflows that include previewing your NFT and tracking royalties. Minimum costs are generally the required gas fees and occasionally a listing fee, which can range from a few dollars to over $100 when network traffic is high. Time investment centers on creation, listing, and occasional promotion. Strong customer support, fraud protection, and clear dashboards help newcomers manage their NFT income and sales effectively.

These methods increase in both complexity and income potential as investor familiarity and involvement deepen, preparing participants for greater opportunities and corresponding risks that follow.

RISK MANAGEMENT, SECURITY, AND PRACTICAL ACTIONS FOR CRYPTO INCOME

Before entering the world of cryptocurrency investing, understanding the basic risks and security requirements is a necessity. Cryptocurrency trades 24/7 and often operates without the regulatory oversight found in traditional finance, making asset protection a core responsibility for individual investors. Market participants face unique threats alongside the promise of high returns, and success starts with building a solid defensive approach.

The variety of scams and risks in the crypto space is striking. Rug pulls — where developers abandon projects and abscond with investors' funds — remain one of the most damaging. In 2021 alone, more than $2.8 billion was lost to rug pulls, with notorious examples like the Squid Game token wiping out millions within hours. Phishing attacks are widespread, targeting individuals through fake emails, direct messages on platforms like Discord or Telegram, and malicious websites that mimic legitimate crypto portals. If a user unknowingly enters their wallet information or seed phrase, their entire wallet can be drained within moments. Pump-and-dump schemes also prevail, particularly in lesser-known tokens, where small groups use social media hype to drive prices up before selling, leaving retail investors with worthless coins. These schemes often gain traction within Telegram groups or Reddit threads, using fake endorsements and fabricated price targets.

Crypto asset values can swing dramatically within short timeframes, which magnifies risk. For instance, during May 2021's market crash, Bitcoin dropped over 30% in a single day, and altcoins saw even deeper slides. Price volatility stems from factors including market speculation, regulatory news, and the influence of major holders known as whales. New investors are often surprised by how little it can take — a rumor, a tweet, or a hacker's declaration — to send prices soaring or crashing.

Red flags in crypto projects are tangible and can be systematically checked. Lack of publicly available white papers means an absence of technical vision or planning. Anonymous or unverified team members should immediately spark skepticism, as transparency is a key marker of legitimacy. Promises of guaranteed returns, rapid multiplication of investments, and suspiciously high staking rewards usually signal unsustainable models or outright scams. Avoid project websites that don't have a clear use case or are overflowing with poor content. Investors are urged to research extensively: reading through documentation, checking developers' history on platforms like GitHub, and examining audit reports from reputable firms.

Protecting digital assets relies on understanding where and how cryptocurrencies are stored. Hot wallets, such as MetaMask, are applications or browser extensions that keep private keys online, offering instant access for daily transactions and decentralized applications. MetaMask simplifies connecting to platforms like Uniswap or OpenSea, but its internet connection exposes it to phishing and malware threats.

For safer storage, cold wallets such as hardware devices — Ledger Nano X and Trezor Model T are industry leaders — keep private keys offline, out of reach from online threats. These tools act like digital safes; funds only leave when the user physically connects the device and confirms the transaction. Best practices for all wallets include storing seed phrases offline on paper, never sharing them or saving them in cloud storage, and enabling two-factor authentication via dedicated apps like Google Authenticator. Using unique, complex passwords and changing them regularly adds another layer of protection.

Long-term holding of trusted cryptocurrencies — commonly called HODLing — minimizes exposure to short-term volatility and speculative risks. Bitcoin (BTC) and Ethereum (ETH) are foundational assets due to their adoption and strong developer communities. Solana (SOL) and Cardano (ADA) present additional opportunities, with beginner-friendly ecosystems and active development. By holding rather than trading frequently, investors sidestep emotional mistakes like panic-selling during a dip or speculative buying on a spike, two actions known for decimating portfolios.

A first practical step is downloading MetaMask for hot storage (for interacting with DeFi platforms) and purchasing a Ledger device for storing significant assets long-term. When setting up these wallets, it is essential to record the seed phrase by hand and store it in a secure, offline location. Enabling device-level two-factor authentication and keeping wallet software updated reduces the attack surface further. For monitoring holdings and prices, tools like CoinGecko, Blockfolio, and Zerion offer tracking across multiple blockchains and wallets without exposing private keys. Portfolio tracking applications provide consolidated overviews, enabling smarter decisions.

Evaluating new projects requires a checklist approach. Confirm the legitimacy of the team by researching LinkedIn profiles or matching GitHub history. Examine tokenomics: check for unfair initial allocations or small circulating supply versus total supply. Review audit reports from established firms such as CertiK or Quantstamp. Assess the transparency and frequency of communication via official channels like Twitter, forums, and Discord. If any stage reveals inconsistencies or evasiveness, the risk is usually unjustifiable.

Investors who set up strong security defenses, manage risks methodically, and research thoroughly position themselves to explore the opportunities in crypto while safeguarding their assets against common and costly threats.

Now that we know the main ways to earn passive income with crypto — staking, yield farming, airdrops, and NFTs — and understand the need for careful risk management and security, new investors can more responsibly explore this changing field. By carefully researching these opportunities, putting in place strong protections, and having realistic expectations about ups and downs and possible scams, readers can confidently start to create a variety of income sources from blockchain. This foundational knowledge empowers entrepreneurs and side hustlers to take their first practical steps toward integrating crypto into a broader strategy for financial independence and long-term wealth creation.

SIX
RENTAL PROPERTIES AND REAL ESTATE CASH FLOW

Picture getting your first rental check and finding that it covers more than the mortgage — an extra monthly income without any work. For many aspiring investors, this moment represents the promise of financial freedom, yet the road to consistent cash flow can be confusing. Questions arise about whether to buy or lease, how to measure profitability, and how much time managing tenants and property upkeep will demand. With so many options and potential pitfalls, beginners often feel overwhelmed before even making their first move.

This chapter will take you through the essential concepts needed to understand rental properties as a source of passive income. You will learn how to evaluate different types of deals, calculate returns with simple financial metrics, and explore strategies that fit various budgets and goals. Additionally, it will guide you through methods of managing these investments efficiently, including ways to automate routine tasks and decide when professional help is worthwhile. The goal is to equip you with clear knowledge so you can approach rental property investing confidently — even if you are just starting out.

EVALUATING DEALS: BUYING VS LEASING AND CASH FLOW ANALYSIS

Rental property investing generally centers on two powerful approaches. The buy-and-hold strategy involves purchasing real estate to own and rent for the long term, benefiting from monthly rental income and value appreciation over years. Lease arbitrage, on the other hand, skips property ownership. Here, an investor signs a long-term lease and sublets the property, often on short-term rental platforms, keeping the difference between rental income and costs.

Buy-and-hold's clear advantages include long-term wealth, steady cash flow, the ability to leverage equity, and favorable tax benefits like depreciation. However, this approach ties up more cash, carries market risk, and faces tenant turnover or property damage. Returns often come from monthly cash flow — say, collecting $2,000 in rent on a property with $1,500 in expenses yields $500 monthly. Over years, appreciation can add significantly more to your net worth. Typical annual returns range from 8% to 15% or more, factoring in both income and appreciation.

Lease arbitrage's allure lies in lower upfront investment since no purchase is needed. Entry is easier — sublease a $1,400/month apartment, furnish it, then top $2,400/month from short-term bookings. Investors pocket the $1,000/month margin after costs. Risks here include landlord restrictions, changing short-term rental regulations, and high vacancy rates. Returns can be high in the short term, but ongoing management is demanding, and there's no equity or appreciation gain. Annualized returns based on cash invested can easily exceed 30%, though volatility is higher.

Accessing these investments starts with traditional financing — mortgages require 15-25% down for single-family rentals, so a $250,000 home might need a $50,000 down payment plus closing costs. Credit score, income, and reserve requirements apply. Creative avenues like seller financing let the buyer make payments directly to the seller, sometimes with less strict approval and lower down payments. Partnerships allow splitting costs and responsibilities — one partner brings cash, the other finds and manages the deal. Joint ventures or syndication structures allow pooling funds, reducing individual capital needed.

Alternative strategies for those with limited savings include house hacking (renting a multi-unit property and living in one unit, letting other tenants cover expenses) or co-signing lease arbitrage arrangements with minimal startup cash.

Successful rental investment requires grasping key financial metrics. The cap rate, or capitalization rate, measures return on investment, excluding financing. If a property costs $200,000 and generates a net income of $16,000 per year after expenses, then the cap rate is calculated as $16,000 divided by $200,000, which equals 8%. Cash-on-cash return considers financing — if you invest $40,000 (down payment and closing costs) and annual cash flow is $6,000, your cash-on-cash profit is $6,000 ÷ $40,000 = 15%. Gross rent multiplier (GRM) quickly compares properties — divide property price by annual rent. A $240,000 property that rents for $2,000/month ($24,000/year) has a GRM of 10; lower GRMs often signal better deals.

Common Rental Expenses Breakdown

Expense Category	Example Monthly Amount	Notes
Mortgage Payment	$1,050	Includes principal & interest.
Property Taxes	$220	Varies by location
Insurance	$80	Landlord policy
Property Management	$160	Usually 8% of rent
Maintenance Reserves	$100	For repairs and vacancies
Utilities	$100	If owner-paid
HOA/Other Fees	$55	If applicable
Total	**$1,765**	

Case Study 1: High-Cash-Flow Property

A duplex in Cleveland purchased for $150,000 rents for $2,200/month. Expenses include a $900 mortgage, $150 in taxes, $75 in insurance, $100 in management, and $125 in reserves/utilities ($1,350 total). Monthly cash flow: $2,200 - $1,350 = $850 ($10,200/year). When an investment of $37,500 is made, the cash-on-cash return is calculated as $10,200 divided by $37,500, resulting in 27.2%. Appreciation may be minimal, but cash flow is strong.

Case Study 2: Strong Appreciation Potential

A Phoenix home costs $400,000 and rents for $2,200/month. Total expenses run $1,950, for a slimmer $250 monthly cash flow ($3,000/year). With $80,000 down, cash-on-cash return is 3.75%. However, if property value grows 6% annually, the house is worth $424,000 after one year, adding $24,000 in unrealized gain. Combined with cash flow, total return for year one is $27,000 ÷ $80,000 = 33.75%.

Establishing passive income requires thoughtful system setup from the beginning. Investors automate rent collection, schedule reminders for maintenance, and set up accounting software like Stessa or AppFolio for bookkeeping. Virtual assistants handle communications, property managers oversee day-to-day operations, and contractors remain on call for repairs. Landlords create onboarding checklists for tenants, standardize screening, and use cloud-based document storage. A well-aligned team includes property managers, bookkeepers, legal advisors, and leasing agents — each ensuring the owner's time commitment stays low.

By linking acquisition strategies, financing, and detailed analysis with disciplined property management and automation, investors build solid pipelines for returns and continuous growth, no matter the market's direction.

MANAGING, AUTOMATING, AND SCALING RENTAL PROPERTY INCOME

Owning rental property can deliver steady passive income with the right management approach. Investors face a pivotal choice: self-managing or hiring a professional property manager. Self-managing cuts costs but increases time and responsibility. Owners oversee marketing, tenant screening, rent collection, maintenance, legal compliance, and financial reporting. Typical out-of-pocket costs include advertising ($100 per listing), background checks ($30 per applicant), and repairs. Investors often spend 4–8 hours per unit monthly handling tenant requests, bookkeeping, and problem-solving.

Professional property managers handle marketing, screening, lease agreements, rent collection, maintenance coordination, and regulatory compliance. Standard industry fees range from 8 to 12% of monthly rent. For a $2,000/month property, expect $160–$240 in management fees plus tenant placement or leasing fees (often equal to one month's rent). Managers often mark up maintenance charges by 10–20% and may add small annual fees for inspections and renewals. This structure reduces owner involvement to oversight and decision-making but cuts into monthly cash flow.

Management Approach	Avg Cost	Owner's Time (per unit/month)	Responsibilities
Self-Manage	$130–$400	4–8 hours	All
Professional PM	$200–$260+	<1 hour	Oversight only

Industry examples show property managers like Greystar or Mynd offering digital portals for owners and tenants. Basic service packages typically include rent collection, maintenance coordination, and financial reporting, with add-ons for eviction handling or 24/7 support.

Digital tools streamline self-management. Tenant screening platforms — like Avail and RentSpree — run criminal, credit, and eviction checks instantly. Users invite tenants to apply online, assess standardized reports, and avoid fair housing violations with uniform criteria. Online rent collection systems such as Apartments.com and PayRent automate reminders, deposits, and late fee enforcement. Funds transfer in 1–3 business days, and tenants use ACH, credit, or debit cards.

Maintenance software — like Buildium and AppFolio — organizes service requests and dispatches vendors. Tenants submit issues online, owners approve work, and the system tracks costs for accounting. Document management tools, such as Dropbox or DocuSign, centralize leases, renewals, and legal notices. Financial tracking apps, including Stessa and QuickBooks, sync with bank accounts, categorize expenses, and generate profit/loss statements for each property.

Short-term rental investors boost efficiency with targeted automation. Smart lock systems (e.g., August, Schlage Encode) enable remote guest access. Owners create temporary codes that expire after checkout, reducing key hand-offs and enhancing security. Dynamic pricing tools like PriceLabs and Beyond optimize nightly rates based on market trends, occupancy, and special events, increasing revenue. Booking calendars on Airbnb, Vrbo, and Booking.com synchronize with channel managers such as Hostfully, eliminating double-bookings and manual updates. Automated messaging tools (Hospitable, AirGMS) schedule check-in instructions, reminders, and responses to guest questions. Cleaning platforms (TurnoverBnB) notify service providers of new reservations, set schedules, and process payments, ensuring units are ready after each stay.

Rental property owners enjoy several tax benefits. Mortgage interest payments on investment properties are fully deductible each year. For instance, a $1,800/month payment on a $350,000 loan can yield over $10,000 in annual interest deductions. Depreciation deductions allow owners to offset rental income by dividing the property's purchase price (minus land value) by 27.5 years. A $330,000 property with $30,000 attributed to land creates a $10,909/year deduction. A 1031 exchange defers capital gains taxes by swapping one property for another. For example, selling a $400,000 rental and buying a $500,000 property avoids immediate taxable gains if IRS timelines and requirements are met. Operating expenses — repairs, property management fees, utilities, and insurance — reduce taxable income; detailed receipts and logs maximize deductions.

The BRRRR method lets investors rapidly expand their portfolios. The five steps are: buy undervalued property; rehab to increase value; rent to a qualified tenant; refinance based on improved appraisal; and repeat using freed-up equity. For example, an investor purchases a fixer-upper for $180,000 and puts $30,000 in repairs, raising the value to $260,000. Renting it for $2,200/month meets lender requirements. Refinancing at 75% loan-to-value nets a $195,000 loan. Subtracting the original loan and rehab recovers initial capital to invest again.

Key BRRRR Calculations

- After-Repair Value (ARV): Property's value post-renovation, validated by recent sales
- Rehab and closing costs must not exceed the difference between the purchase price and the after-repair value (ARV), after accounting for equity requirements.
- Cash-Out: New loan amount (typically 70–75% of ARV) minus payoff and costs equals available funds

Timelines average 4–7 months from purchase to refinance; delays can occur from lengthy rehabs or tenant placement. Risks include underestimated repairs, low appraisals, and high vacancy. Successful BRRRRs require conservative calculations, skilled contractors, and reliable tenants.

Rental income steadily pays down mortgages, increasing owner equity and net worth. For example, if a property generates $900/month in positive cash flow, the owner accumulates $54,000 over five years, along with equity from principal paydown and appreciation. Repeating this process with multiple properties multiplies returns and enables faster acquisitions using new cash-out refinances.

Choosing property management methods and using automation tools makes work easier, improves tenant happiness, and boosts passive income — through clear actions that investors can start right away.

Now that we understand the fundamentals of evaluating rental property deals, generating positive cash flow, and effectively managing or automating operations, aspiring investors are equipped to confidently build a strong foundation for passive income. By applying careful financial analysis, choosing suitable acquisition strategies, and leveraging technology or professional management, beginners can minimize risks and maximize returns. This knowledge paves the way for scaling a profitable rental business portfolio that steadily grows wealth and supports long-term financial independence, empowering readers to take actionable steps toward escaping traditional work constraints and creating lasting economic freedom.

SEVEN
REITS - REAL ESTATE INVESTING WITHOUT PROPERTY

Have you ever wanted to invest in real estate but felt overwhelmed by the thought of buying property, managing tenants, or dealing with maintenance issues? The idea of earning steady income from buildings and land is appealing, yet many hesitate because traditional property investment comes with its set of challenges and demands. For someone balancing a busy career or exploring ways to build passive income streams, owning physical real estate may seem out of reach or too time-consuming.

Real estate has long been considered a powerful way to generate wealth and secure financial freedom. However, the hands-on nature of property ownership can limit who benefits from this asset class. Many aspiring investors search for methods that allow them to participate in the real estate market without the complexities of direct ownership. This raises questions about how one can gain exposure to real estate's income and growth potential while maintaining flexibility and minimizing effort.

This chapter explores Real Estate Investment Trusts (REITs), investment vehicles designed to make real estate accessible, liquid, and beginner-friendly. It discusses the different types of REITs, how they function, and why they have become popular among those looking for stable dividend income without the headaches of managing physical properties. Additionally, it offers guidance on building diversified portfolios tailored to various risk tolerances and income goals. By understanding REITs, readers will find practical strategies to incorporate real estate into their passive income plans, moving closer to financial independence with a manageable and flexible approach.

UNDERSTANDING REITS AND THEIR TYPES

A Real Estate Investment Trust, commonly known as a REIT, is a company that owns, operates, or finances income-generating real estate. Unlike buying a single home or apartment, investing in a REIT lets a person own a small part of a much larger mix of properties. The properties can include office buildings, shopping malls, apartment complexes, hotels, and even hospitals. The main idea is similar to the way a mutual fund operates. works, except that instead of buying bonds or stocks, a REIT pools together money from many investors to invest in real estate.

REITs are unique because of a legal structure that requires them by law to pay out at least 90% of their taxable income each year as dividends to shareholders. This rule, set by the U.S. Congress in 1960, was intended to give ordinary people a way to benefit from real estate income without needing to buy actual property themselves. For example, if a REIT earns $10 million in taxable income in a year, it must distribute at least $9 million as dividends. This high payout requirement is one reason why REITs are attractive for people looking to earn passive income. Many REITs have dividend yields between 4% and 8% per year, meaning that investing $1,000 could generate $40–$80 in annual dividends, which is often higher than what is paid by traditional stocks.

There are three main forms of REITs, each working a little differently. Equity REITs are the most common. These own and manage real estate themselves, collecting rent from tenants and making money as the value of the properties goes up over time. For instance, a well-known equity REIT like Simon Property Group owns shopping centers and malls. Another example is AvalonBay Communities, which owns and manages thousands of apartment buildings across the United States. These companies earn most of their money from rent payments.

Mortgage REITs, or mREITs, do not own real estate directly. Instead, they own or buy mortgages and real estate loans. They make money by earning interest on these mortgages, rather than collecting rent. Annaly Capital Management is one of the largest mREITs and invests in home mortgage-backed securities. Because Mortgage REITs depend on interest rates and loan payments, their income can be more sensitive to changes in the economy.

Hybrid REITs combine both approaches. They own physical properties like an equity REIT and also invest in mortgages like a Mortgage REIT. Starwood Property Trust is a real-world example. By mixing both strategies, Hybrid REITs try to balance the benefits and risks of owning buildings and providing real estate financing.

Investors choose REITs for several important benefits. First, REITs are generally very liquid. Unlike apartments or commercial buildings, which can take months or years to sell, investors can buy or sell shares in publicly traded REITs instantly during market hours on a stock exchange, just like other stocks. For example, if an investor needs cash, they could sell $500 worth of REIT shares in seconds, while it would take much longer to sell a piece of real property.

REITs add diversification to an investment portfolio. Factors like company profits or interest rates affect stocks and bonds, but real estate often moves differently. In 2022, the average 20-year annualized return on U.S. Equity REITs was about 9.9%, which can offer a meaningful counterbalance to other assets. This diversification can help reduce overall risk.

Another strength is the low minimum investment required. While buying a single property could take a down payment of $20,000 or more, investors can start with REITs for as little as the price of one share, often under $100. Some platforms even offer fractional investing, making ownership even more accessible to new investors.

There are key differences between public and private REITs. Publicly traded REITs are listed on stock exchanges like the New York Stock Exchange or NASDAQ. This makes them easy to buy and sell, and their prices are updated every second while markets are open. They are subject to strict regulation by the Securities and Exchange Commission (SEC) and must report their financials regularly, making them more transparent. Anyone with a brokerage account can invest in public REITs.

Private REITs, by contrast, are not traded on public markets. They are usually available only to institutional investors or high-net-worth individuals. Private REITs tend to be less liquid, sometimes requiring years before an investor can sell their shares. They have fewer reporting requirements and are less strictly regulated, so investors may have less information about their operations. This makes private REITs potentially more volatile and risky, but occasionally they offer higher returns to compensate for these extra risks.

The variety of REIT types, public or private, and their different structures give investors many options to choose from, based on their risk tolerance, goals, and preferences for passive income generation.

BUILDING AND EVALUATING A DIVERSIFIED REIT PORTFOLIO

Portfolio Construction Method

Start by defining your "freedom number." This is the amount of passive income you plan to generate per month. Build your portfolio so projected dividends cover or exceed this target. Select your strategy based on risk tolerance, income needs, and time horizon. Use the following risk-based models as guides, all using a $100,000 starting capital:

Conservative Model: Income Focus

- **Sector Allocation:**
- Residential: 40%
- Healthcare: 25%

- Commercial/Office: 20%
- Data Centers/Infrastructure: 15%
- **Sample Holdings:**
- Vanguard Real Estate ETF (VNQ): 40%
- Welltower Inc. (WELL): 15%
- Realty Income (O): 15%
- Public Storage (PSA): 10%
- Digital Realty (DLR): 10%
- Prologis (PLD): 10%
- **Expected Yield:** 4-5.5%
- **Risk Level:** Low
- **Holding Period:** 5+ years
- **Rebalancing:** Every 12 months

Balanced Model: Moderate Growth and Income

- **Sector Allocation:**
- Residential: 30%
- Retail/Commercial: 30%
- Healthcare: 15%
- Data Centers/Infrastructure: 25%
- **Sample Holdings:**
- Schwab U.S. REIT ETF (SCHH): 30%
- Simon Property Group (SPG): 20%
- Prologis (PLD): 15%
- Equinix (EQIX): 15%
- Welltower (WELL): 10%
- Digital Realty (DLR): 10%
- **Expected Yield:** 3.5-4.5%
- **Risk Level:** Medium
- **Holding Period:** 3-5 years
- **Rebalancing:** Every 6 months

Aggressive Model: Growth Emphasis

- **Sector Allocation:**
- Data Centers/Infrastructure: 40%
- Industrial/Logistics: 25%
- Specialty (Cell Towers, Self-Storage): 20%
- Residential/Healthcare: 15%
- **Sample Holdings:**
- iShares Cohen & Steers REIT ETF (ICF): 30%
- American Tower (AMT): 25%
- Prologis (PLD): 20%
- CubeSmart (CUBE): 10%
- Invitation Homes (INVH): 10%
- Ventas Inc. (VTR): 5%
- **Expected Yield:** 2.5-3.5%
- **Risk Level:** High
- **Holding Period:** 5+ years
- **Rebalancing:** Every 4 months

Use dollar-cost averaging by investing a fixed amount monthly (for example, $1,000/month split among selections above). This smooths out price fluctuations and helps avoid market timing mistakes.

Monthly income portfolios prioritize high-dividend, stable REITs, while growth portfolios allocate more to sectors and REITs with historically stronger appreciation. Adjust allocation on your portfolio worksheet to see how changes affect projected monthly income versus total value growth.

Portfolio Model	Target Yield	Income Focus	Growth Focus	Recommended ETF
Conservative	4–5.5%	High	Low	VNQ, WELL, O
Balanced	3.5–4.5%	Medium	Medium	SCHH, SPG, DLR
Aggressive	2.5–3.5%	Low	High	ICF, AMT, PLD

REIT Evaluation Framework

Evaluate each candidate REIT with consistent, objective criteria. Prioritize total return (dividends + growth) as it relates to your freedom number.

Key Metrics to Track:

- **Funds From Operations (FFO):** Measures recurring cash flow. Choose REITs with rising or steady FFO per share.
- **Dividend Yield:** Annual dividend divided by current price; look for sustainable yields above the REIT sector average.
- **Payout Ratio:** Portion of FFO paid as dividends; 70–90% usually signals stability without limiting growth.

Sector Considerations:

- Residential and healthcare usually deliver steady income. Retail and industrial reflect economic cycles more strongly. Data centers and infrastructure offer growth but can be more volatile.

Sector	Typical Yield	Stability	Growth Potential
Residential	3–4%	High	Moderate
Retail/Commercial	4–6%	Medium	Variable
Healthcare	3.5–5%	High	Moderate
Data Centers	2–3.5%	Medium	High
Specialty	2–4%	Medium	High

Market Cycle Analysis:

Assess local and national real estate trends, vacancy rates, and whether rents are rising or falling. In expansion phases, growth REITs outperform. For late-cycle conditions, shift the portfolio towards sectors with long-term leases (healthcare, residential).

Comprehensive Tools and Frameworks:

- **REIT Scorecard:** Assign scores (1–5) for FFO growth, dividend safety, management quality, and sector risk.
- **Diversification Matrix:** Tally sector exposure to avoid overconcentration.
- **Income Calculator:** Multiply shares held by expected dividend per share to see monthly income.
- **Risk Checklist:** Review leverage (debt/equity), sector risk, and geographic diversification before finalizing allocations.

Case Studies

Investor Type	Sample Holdings	Allocation	Expected Annual Income	Growth Projection
Retiree	VNQ, WELL, O, PSA, DLR	40%/15%/15%/10%/10%/10%	$4,800 (4.8% yield)	Low
Professional	SCHH, SPG, PLD, EQIX, WELL, DLR	30%/20%/15%/15%/10%/10%	$4,100 (4.1% yield)	Moderate
Young Investor	ICF, AMT, PLD, CUBE, INVH, VTR	30%/25%/20%/10%/10%/5%	$2,800 (2.8% yield)	High

Calculate progress monthly to track how close you are to your freedom number. Rebalance allocations as needed, using your risk checklist and updated market data, to maintain the right mix and pursue financial independence efficiently.

Now that we have explored the fundamentals of Real Estate Investment Trusts and how to build a diversified portfolio tailored to different risk levels and income goals, readers are equipped to confidently incorporate REITs into their passive income strategies. By understanding the unique benefits of REITs — such as liquidity, dividend payouts, and exposure to various property sectors — aspiring investors can make informed choices that align with their personal financial freedom targets. With practical frameworks for evaluating and balancing REIT holdings, this knowledge serves as a strong foundation to steadily grow passive income, reduce reliance on traditional employment, and move closer to achieving long-term financial independence.

EIGHT
DROPSHIPPING AND E-COMMERCE AUTOMATION

Starting an online business without holding inventory has become an increasingly attractive option for many aspiring entrepreneurs. The idea of running a store that sells products without the need to stock or ship them personally offers a promise of flexibility and scalability. Yet, behind this appealing model lies a complex web of decisions — from choosing the right products to marketing effectively and automating operations — that can be overwhelming to navigate.

This chapter will guide readers through the essential steps of building such a business. It covers how to identify profitable products, establish an efficient online storefront, and implement automation tools that reduce manual work. Additionally, it explores strategies for scaling the business while maintaining smooth operations and delivering excellent customer service. By understanding these elements, readers can create a passive income stream through dropshipping and e-commerce with greater confidence and clarity.

FINDING PROFITABLE PRODUCTS AND BUILDING YOUR STORE

Choosing the right niche forms the backbone of any successful dropshipping venture. A profitable niche isn't just about what's trending — it's about solving real problems or addressing clear desires within a particular group. For example, instead of broadly selling "kitchen supplies," targeting "eco-friendly kitchen products for busy parents" reaches a more specific group who cares about both sustainability and convenience. Another focused niche might be "pet care solutions for apartment dwellers," recognizing the unique needs of people who want to care for pets in smaller, urban environments.

A strong niche typically meets several criteria, including a specific customer profile, a clear problem or desire, and space for unique value. Imagine someone who loves to hike but struggles to find minimalist, lightweight gear for quick day trips. If existing brands cater mostly to advanced adventures with heavy gear, there's an untapped market for simple, affordable solutions.

Market research is essential to discover and test these opportunities. Google Trends is a valuable starting point; searching "reusable produce bags" over time can reveal steady or rising interest, indicating growing consumer awareness. If searches jump during certain months, like before summer farmers' markets, it can signal a seasonal peak. Reviewing Amazon Best Sellers for related categories shows what's in demand right now. Exploring "Home & Kitchen" might reveal top-selling silicone bags for food storage. Analyze their reviews — do customers mention missing features or frustrations? These are opportunities to improve on existing offerings.

On TikTok, viral products often signal future trends. Searching for hashtags such as #EcoKitchen or #PetApartmentHacks uncovers what creators and audiences are buzzing about. If several videos highlighting collapsible water bowls for dogs gain hundreds of thousands of views, this points to strong engagement and shareability. AliExpress Hot Products can help spot emerging bestsellers. Filter categories, sort by order volume, and scan recent reviews to grasp real customer experiences and whether the interest is new or saturated.

After market research, use a consistent product validation process to filter high-potential ideas. Start with demand indicators: check Google search volume via free keyword tools, tally Amazon review counts, and track TikTok or Instagram likes and comments per product type. A threshold like 5,000 searches per month for "eco-friendly lunch bags" signals healthy curiosity.

Competition analysis comes next. Is the Amazon results page packed with nearly identical listings with thousands of reviews each? High saturation means higher advertising costs and tougher differentiation. Look for gaps, like only a few brands offering machine-washable or fully biodegradable materials.

Profit margin calculations are essential to avoid products that look good but barely earn anything. For example, let's say eco-lunch bags cost $4 per unit on AliExpress, including shipping, and average $18 on Amazon. After subtracting about 15% in Amazon fees ($2.70) and leaving a buffer for marketing ($2.00), there's roughly $9.30 left. This is over 50% gross margin, which is healthy for a dropshipping product.

Shipping times directly affect customer satisfaction. Use supplier dashboards that display estimated delivery to target regions. If most customers are in the U.S. and the supplier can only deliver in 25–40 days, the product is much harder to automate and maintain. Prefer suppliers with local warehouses or ePacket/express options, keeping shipping under two weeks if possible.

Quality matters for long-term viability. Order samples or look for detailed photo reviews showing the product in real use. If several users complain about leaks or rapid wear of the product, "eco-friendly lunch bags," reconsider or source alternative suppliers. Devoting attention to product presentation, packaging, and branding also helps set apart similar offers from your competition.

When exploring potential pitfalls, market saturation is a frequent challenge. Run simple counts: if a niche returns dozens of similar top sellers and every Google ad is packed with familiar names, reconsider or look for a tighter sub-niche. To avoid generic products, focus on bundle deals ("starter kits" with unique add-ons), partnerships with micro-influencers, or custom packaging with personal notes. Brand positioning can hinge on visual storytelling: "We help city dog lovers keep pets healthy in apartments with space-saving, eco-smart essentials."

Validating a product might look like this: researching collapsible pet water bowls, you see 15,000 monthly global searches, three Amazon sellers with fewer than 200 reviews, a $4.90 landed cost, and a $17–$19 customer price. Social media reveals high engagement rates, and supplier review photos show quality. Shipping from a U.S. warehouse is available, averaging 5–8 days. These factors suggest a viable product with healthy margins and differentiation space.

E-commerce platforms offer different strengths. Shopify is popular for its drag-and-drop site builder, integration with apps like Oberlo, and transparent monthly pricing. It's scalable but has fees for premium features. WooCommerce plugs into WordPress, boasts flexibility and low upfront costs, but demands more technical know-how. Wix and BigCommerce aim for beginners, with simple storefront editors but fewer automation tools. Each platform links to dropshipping apps for product import, automatic stock updates, order forwarding, and tracking notifications. Choosing a platform that easily connects these tools is crucial for minimizing manual work and creating a business that runs smoothly with little intervention — setting the stage for true automation.

AUTOMATING OPERATIONS AND SCALING YOUR BUSINESS

When a dropshipping operation is ready to scale, transforming day-to-day management into a largely hands-off process hinges on intentional automation and effective outsourcing. Store owners quickly realize that managing everything manually isn't sustainable as order volume rises. Instead, integrating smart automated systems will free up time, reduce errors, and enable strategic focus on growth.

The first layer is automating order fulfillment. Apps like Oberlo, DSers, and AutoDS connect directly with your e-commerce platform, syncing orders as they're placed. These tools automatically send order details to suppliers, track shipment status, update customers with tracking numbers, and flag inventory shortages in real time. For instance, a

Shopify store using DSers can set up rules to auto-route orders to the optimal supplier and instantly notify customers at each fulfillment stage. Store owners can set inventory alerts to prompt reordering or temporarily pause advertising for products running low.

Customer service, often a bottleneck in scaling, can be largely automated. Chatbots like Tidio or Gorgias answer common questions — shipping times, order status, return policies — instantly, 24/7. Automated email systems, set up within platforms like Klaviyo or Mailchimp, provide tailored responses to inquiries such as shipping updates, refund processes, or account support. A ticket management solution like Zendesk funnels messages from all channels and auto-assigns them based on category and urgency. For more complex queries, clearly defined protocols empower virtual assistants (VAs) to resolve issues efficiently. Building a guide on when to escalate, how to issue refunds, and template responses for frequent situations ensures consistent customer experiences even as the support team grows or shifts.

Standard Operating Procedures (SOPs) underpin systematization. Developing SOPs for each core area — product listing, order processing, customer communication, returns, and dispute resolution — removes ambiguity and speeds up onboarding. For product listings, a step-by-step document defines image requirements, keyword integration, category mapping, and pricing formulas. Order processing SOPs cover everything from verifying details, pushing requests to suppliers, confirming fulfillment in the backend, and escalating backorders. Create standardized scripts for customer support covering inquiries, complaints, and refunds. Returns and dispute SOPs should clarify timelines, evidence requirements, and refund approvals. Storing these guidelines in a shared drive and maintaining a log of updates lets new VAs quickly become effective contributors.

To accelerate revenue, paid advertising automation becomes essential. With Facebook Ads, create targeted campaigns using lookalike audiences from past customers, set daily budget caps, and use rules that pause underperforming ads automatically. A good benchmark is aiming for a Return on Ad Spend (ROAS) of at least 3.0. On Google

Shopping campaigns, group products by margin and set custom bidding strategies, leveraging automated bid adjustments. TikTok Ads benefit from creative A/B testing — run at least three video variants at a time, track click-through and conversion rates, then reallocate budget to top performers. Use tools like AdEspresso for managing cross-platform ad experiments and tracking ROAS in real time. Continuous split-testing of ad copy, creative, and audience targeting ensures money is spent where returns are highest.

Influencer marketing can be streamlined for scale. Start by filtering Instagram and TikTok micro-influencers whose audience matches your niche, using platforms like Influence.co or Upfluence. A successful outreach template might read: "Hi [Name], we love your content! We think your followers would enjoy our [product]. Would you be interested in a paid collaboration or affiliate opportunity?" Set up scalable commission structures, such as offering 10-15% per sale. Track influencer performance via unique promo codes and UTM links in Google Analytics or Refersion. Regularly review conversions per influencer to double down on top performers.

For sustained organic traffic, SEO automation delivers compounding gains. Optimize product titles, descriptions, and meta tags with high-intent keywords discovered using Ahrefs or SEMrush. Use consistent keyword research workflows — identify main terms via competitor analysis and expand with long-tails found through Google Suggest. Build content marketing around buyer guides, FAQs, and evergreen blog posts, scheduling releases with editorial calendars. Technical SEO, such as site speed optimization, structured data, and mobile responsiveness checks, can be monitored with plugins and Google Search Console.

Email marketing can run on autopilot while nurturing revenue. Abandoned cart recovery flows trigger a sequence of three emails urging completion, often recapturing 15-20% of lost sales — set these in Shopify, Klaviyo, or Omnisend. Post-purchase upsell sequences offer related products or incentives within a week of the initial order. A welcoming series introduces new subscribers, shares brand values, and highlights bestsellers over 5-7 short messages. Retention campaigns send personalized offers every few months based on browsing or purchase data.

Case in point, an apparel dropshipper implemented Klaviyo's prebuilt flows and recovered $15,000/month in abandoned carts while using Gorgias chatbots to cut live agent shifts by 40%. Across all systems, monitor key metrics — order error rates, average reply times, support ticket resolution, and ad ROI. Routinely map, test, and refine each workflow, doubling down on what delivers an efficient, profitable, hands-off business.

Now that you understand how to identify profitable products, build an automated dropshipping store, and scale operations through smart marketing and efficient outsourcing, you are well-equipped to create a passive income stream that requires minimal hands-on management. By focusing on targeted niches, validating product demand, leveraging e-commerce platforms, and embracing automation tools, you can move beyond traditional work constraints toward financial independence. The next step is to apply these strategies consistently, refine your systems over time, and expand your online business steadily — transforming initial efforts into sustainable, scalable income that supports your broader journey to freedom and wealth diversification.

NINE
CREATING AND MONETIZING A YOUTUBE CHANNEL

Starting a YouTube channel can feel overwhelming, especially when you don't know where to begin or worry about being on camera. Many aspiring creators struggle with uncertainty about which topics will attract viewers consistently and how to turn their efforts into lasting income. The challenge grows when trends change rapidly and content loses relevance quickly, leaving creators frustrated as their channels stall or fail to generate steady revenue.

For those who prefer to work behind the scenes or are new to video creation, building a channel that earns passive income might seem out of reach. Questions about choosing the right niche, producing videos that continue to draw attention over time, and finding effective ways to monetize can create doubt. It's easy to wonder how others succeed in this space while feeling stuck trying to get started without the pressure of constant content updates or expensive equipment.

This chapter addresses these concerns by guiding readers through the process of creating a YouTube channel focused on evergreen topics — subjects that maintain interest and search demand long after the videos are published. It explores how to identify niches with strong income potential, explains key monetization methods beyond just ads, and highlights strategies for using automation and outsourcing to manage growth smoothly. Whether you're camera-shy or just beginning your online journey, understanding these principles can open the door to developing a sustainable source of passive income on YouTube.

SELECTING HIGH-POTENTIAL NICHES AND PRODUCING EVERGREEN CONTENT

A passive-friendly YouTube niche centers on topics with enduring interest. Evergreen content never loses its relevance, staying valuable for months or years. Viewers search for these topics consistently, creating opportunities for ongoing ad revenue and low-effort automation. An ideal passive niche allows for prerecorded videos or content scheduled well in advance, without relying on fast-changing trends or news cycles.

Timeless topics include meditation, which appeals to those seeking relaxation or stress management year-round. Personal finance tutorials attract regular search traffic, as viewers always look to improve their budgeting, investing, and financial planning skills. Productivity advice — like time management techniques or organization systems — remains relevant, helping people achieve their goals in any season. Channels offering ambient content such as study music, white noise, and nature sounds enjoy a steady audience, as new viewers always seek these for work or rest. These examples maintain long-term utility, attracting viewers at all times and maximizing passive earning potential.

A systematic approach to niche selection helps filter for profitability and fit. The process begins with identifying personal expertise or authentic interest. Content creators who enjoy their subject have a better chance at consistency and avoiding burnout. For example, someone with experience in budgeting may find personal finance tutorials satisfying and impactful.

Analyzing market demand and competition follows. Using tools like TubeBuddy, creators enter potential keywords related to their topic, such as "budgeting for beginners." TubeBuddy displays search volume statistics and reveals if the keyword is in high demand. VidIQ assists by measuring competitiveness and also showing top-ranking videos in that topic. The ideal scenario is a niche with steady search volume and moderate competition. Highly saturated fields may be harder to penetrate without unique content or a fresh perspective, while topics with low search volume may not sustain ongoing income.

Income potential assessment is a critical filter. Creators measure this by checking metrics such as estimated ad rates and affiliate marketing possibilities. Categories like personal finance, tech, and productivity historically command high CPMs (cost per thousand impressions). For example, personal finance channels on YouTube regularly report CPMs ranging from $15 to $30, significantly higher than entertainment or lifestyle content, which may only offer $2 to $5 CPM. Affiliate marketing also plays a significant role; technology review channels can generate recurring commissions by linking to software or products in descriptions.

A table can help clarify:

Niche	Average CPM ($)	Affiliate Potential	Sponsorship Demand	Evergreen?
Personal Finance	15-30	High	High	Yes
Tech Reviews	8-20	High	High	Yes
Productivity Tips	5-15	Medium	Medium	Yes
Ambient Music/Sounds	1-10	Low	Low	Yes

Monthly search volumes help gauge audience size. For example, the term "guided meditation" averages 100,000–200,000 monthly global searches, while "investment for beginners" registers 30,000–60,000. A target search volume for a profitable evergreen topic is typically between 10,000 and 100,000 searches per month, depending on sub-niche specificity and competition.

KeywordTool.io extracts long-tail versions of high-performing keywords. Typing "budgeting" reveals phrases like "budgeting tips for students" or "budgeting with irregular income," which often face less competition but serve substantial, specific audiences. These variations help carve out unique positioning without sacrificing demand.

Audience engagement signals the viability of a passive niche. Channels with high like-to-view ratios, consistent comments, and positive community feedback are more likely to earn from sponsorships and digital product sales. Educational and finance channels routinely attract brand partnerships and premium online course creation opportunities. For example, finance-focused channels like Graham Stephan's — built on investing insights — leverage affiliate links to stock trading platforms and sponsored integrations, generating passive streams beyond AdSense.

Data illustrates ad revenue potential across niches. Personal finance channels emphasize long watch time per video, driving higher ad views and repeat engagement. Technology channels successfully feature affiliate links for recurring software subscriptions, offering income from both YouTube ads and third-party commissions. Productivity creators bundle digital planners or online courses, further boosting passive earnings. Even ambient channels utilize playlist automation, resulting in continuous advertisements.

A structured process solidifies decision-making:

1. List top interests and expertise areas.
2. Use TubeBuddy, VidIQ, and KeywordTool.io to gauge demand, competition, and keyword opportunities.
3. Research top channels in each niche, observing ad types, affiliate links, and sponsored segments.
4. Compare CPM rates, engagement patterns, and monetization diversity.
5. Select topics that align with personal strengths and the required passive infrastructure — evergreen themes, high CPM, repeat viewing, and automation potential.

By looking at real-life ways to earn passive income with lasting content, creators can see a process based on valuable topics, smart ways to make money, and content that can grow easily. Channels focused on personal finance, tech tutorials, and study music highlight the necessary blend of topic selection, optimization tools, and revenue streams, preparing for sustainable, hands-off growth.

MONETIZING, AUTOMATING, AND SCALING YOUR CHANNEL FOR LONG-TERM SUCCESS

A successful path to YouTube passive income brings several monetization streams together, each stacking onto the last for compounding results. To build a machine that runs almost on autopilot, it's vital to understand the biggest monetization avenues and how they interlock. Start by focusing on the YouTube Partner Program, expand into affiliate links and sponsorships, and set up systems for scaling through automation and outsourcing.

YouTube Partner Program: Foundation of YouTube Revenue

The YouTube Partner Program (YPP) is the formal entry point for ad revenue. You must have at least 1,000 subscribers and either 4,000 valid public watch hours in the past 12 months or 10 million Shorts views in the last 90 days. Meeting these thresholds unlocks ad placements on your videos.

Implementation Steps:

- Enable two-step verification and adhere to all YouTube monetization policies.
- Apply for YPP in YouTube Studio.
- Once approved, monetize videos during upload or for past content.

Earnings Range:

A channel with 100K subscribers and consistent uploads in tech or finance can see $3,000-$5,000+ a month from ads, depending on CPM (cost per thousand impressions), which typically ranges from $2 to $20.

Optimization Tips:

- Place ads after the first 60 seconds for longer videos to boost mid-roll revenue.
- Analyze demographic data; audiences in the US, Canada, and Australia raise CPM.
- Encourage viewers to sign up for YouTube Premium — your channel earns a percentage based on Premium viewers' watch time.

YouTube splits ad revenue 55/45 with creators. For YouTube Premium, revenue comes from a pool, distributed based on watch time, giving a slight boost to channels with longer average viewing durations.

Affiliate Marketing: Expanding Beyond Ads

Affiliate marketing lets you earn a commission when viewers purchase products through special links you share. This is powerful in niches like tech reviews, beauty, and home improvement.

Requirements:

- Program approval from networks such as Amazon Associates, ClickBank, or ShareASale.
- Disclosure compliance (clearly state affiliations in video descriptions).

Steps to Implement:

- Integrate product or offer mentions within relevant videos.
- Pin affiliate links at the top of the description and as a YouTube comment.
- Use trackable link shorteners to monitor clicks and conversions.

Earnings Range:

Commissions range from 1% (Amazon) up to 75%+ (digital products on ClickBank). For example, a finance channel with 50K monthly clicks on credit card affiliate links could earn $2,500 to $10,000+ monthly if 1-2% convert.

Optimization Advice:

- Use callouts and on-screen prompts to guide viewers to descriptions.
- Rotate offers and highlight limited-time deals.

Sponsorships: High-Ticket Monetization

Brand deals provide a more predictable, sizable revenue stream. Companies pay for video mentions, dedicated segments, or entire sponsored videos.

Key Steps:

- Create a media kit (channel stats, audience breakdown, engagement rates).
- Use this formula to estimate rates: $20-$40 per 1,000 views for mid-roll integrations; $100-$200 per 1,000 views for dedicated content.
- Outreach template:
- "Hello [Brand], I'm [Name], creator of [Channel]. I average [X] views per video and have an engaged audience in [Niche]. I'd love to partner with [Brand] for a sponsored segment to

introduce your [Product/Service]. Attached is my media kit for review."

Implementation:

- Track responses, follow up after 7 days, and negotiate deliverables.
- Use platforms like FameBit, Grapevine, or direct email outreach.

A beauty channel securing two $3,000 package deals per month (audience 75K subscribers, high engagement) can reliably add $6,000 to monthly revenue.

Automation and Outsourcing for Scale

Automation reduces repetitive workload and maintains channel consistency:

- **Templates:** Prebuilt video descriptions, affiliate disclaimers, and title formats.
- **Content Calendars:** Use tools like Trello or Notion to map upload dates, sponsorships, and social promo.
- **Scheduling:** Batch-record and upload using YouTube's scheduler or TubeBuddy's bulk processing.
- **Team Management:** Assign video editing, thumbnail design, and community management to freelancers.

Outsourcing Essentials

Role	Typical Budget Per Video	Platform Suggestions
Video Editor	$50-$150	Upwork, Fiverr
Thumbnail Designer	$10-$35	Fiverr, 99designs
Scriptwriter	$40-$120	Upwork, Scripted
Virtual Assistant	$7-$15/hr	OnlineJobs.ph, Upwork

- Set clear guidelines and samples.
- Incorporate weekly quality reviews and audience feedback.

Compounding Revenue and Metrics for Success

Revenue multiplies when ad earnings, affiliate commissions, and sponsorship deals overlap. For instance, the channel "BeatTheBush" began with ad revenue, incorporated Amazon and credit card affiliate links, and subsequently secured sponsorships, resulting in a compound monthly income increase from under $1,500 to over $8,000 over a period of two years. Track your metrics: Target a 10% MoM (month-over-month) revenue lift with each new monetization stream.

The YouTube Automation Starter Kit

The Automation Starter Kit contains customizable description templates, outreach email templates, content calendar formats, recommended outsourcing checklists, and links to must-have tools (TubeBuddy, YouTube Studio bulk actions, and scheduling apps). Download each copy for your channel and deploy immediately as you practice automation and scaling through the next exercises.

Now that we understand how to select high-potential, evergreen niches and apply proven monetization strategies like the YouTube Partner Program, affiliate marketing, and sponsorships, we can confidently build a YouTube channel that generates passive income with minimal ongoing effort. By leveraging smart automation and outsourcing, even beginners or those who are camera-shy can scale their channels efficiently while maintaining consistent quality and audience engagement. This foundation not only opens doors to sustainable, diversified revenue streams but also empowers aspiring entrepreneurs to move closer to financial independence and freedom from traditional work constraints.

TEN
SELLING ONLINE COURSES AND TEACHING WHAT YOU KNOW

Many people possess valuable skills or knowledge they wish to share but feel held back by the technical challenges of creating and selling online courses. The idea of building a digital product that earns income around the clock seems appealing, yet daunting questions arise: Where do I start? How do I find a topic that others want to learn? What if I'm not a professional teacher or tech expert? These uncertainties often prevent potential creators from taking the first step toward turning their expertise into a scalable source of passive income.

In reality, successful online courses are not about delivering endless information; they are about guiding learners through meaningful change. People don't pay for facts — they invest in clear transformations that improve their lives. Whether it's mastering a new skill, overcoming a personal challenge, or achieving a career goal, the demand lies in actionable, proven methods that produce real results. This chapter explores how to identify those transformations within your own experience and create course content that meets a genuine need. It also examines practical options for hosting and selling your course, showing how you can maintain control without needing advanced technical skills. By understanding these core principles, you can build an online course business that grows steadily while freeing you from the limitations of traditional work.

FINDING YOUR COURSE TOPIC AND CREATING EFFECTIVE CONTENT

Imagine a world where knowledge is free, but real change is rare. This is the starting point for creating profitable online courses: transformation is what people pay for, not just more information. Anyone can search for calorie charts or "tips to lose weight." They will pay, however, for a system that helps them shed 20 pounds while working full-time and looking after their kids. Information shows "what." Transformation delivers the "how" — with real, lasting results.

Understanding the Transformation Principle

Consider two scenarios. Someone searches online and finds hundreds of coding tutorials. Most are free. But a complete beginner craving a new career needs more than random videos. They need a step-by-step programming roadmap, showing exactly how to go from no experience to landing a first tech job, with milestones, templates, and feedback. Similarly, while anyone can download a generic meal plan, a course that guides busy parents to create sustainable meal prepping habits while balancing work and children is much more valuable. It solves a more profound problem.

This is the transformation principle: successful courses create clear before-and-after results for learners. The question to ask is not, "What facts do I know?" but, "Where have I created meaningful change in my life or someone else's — and how can I walk others through the same journey?"

Problem-Solution Matrix Exercise

Unlocking your profitable course idea starts with drawing from your wins and challenges. The following framework makes the process practical and focused.

Step 1: List Personal Victories and Challenges Overcome

Begin by reflecting on your experiences. Jot down moments where you faced a challenge and came out on the other side stronger or more skilled. These can relate to work, health, money, relationships, or personal skills.

- Instruction: Write 5-10 experiences where you solved a problem or improved your situation.
- Example entries:
    - Changed careers from nursing to project management
    - Lost 30 pounds through home workouts
    - Learned conversational Spanish in six months
    - Paid off $20,000 in debt
    - Organized a cluttered home office for better productivity
- Validation criteria: The challenge must be common and relatable to others, not just a unique situation.

Step 2: Identify the Transformation Achieved

Now, for each entry, clarify the change that actually took place. What did your "before" look like compared to your "after"?

- Instruction: Describe the starting point and the outcome.
- Example entries:
    - From: Uncertain and burned out in healthcare To: Confident and happy in a new tech role
    - From: Overweight and low energy To: Fit, energetic, and running 5k races
    - From: Daunted by debt To: Debt-free and saving for a home
- Validation criteria: You should be able to express the benefit in clear, plain language.

Step 3: Define the Before and After States

Transformations are most compelling when the contrasts are direct and vivid. Document how life looked "before" and "after" for each achievement.

- Instruction: Use bullet points to draw a line between the before and after.
- Example entries:

Before	After
Disorganized workspace	Calm, productive office space
Struggling to lead team	Confident, effective manager
Confused about budgeting	Consistently saving money

- Validation criteria: The "after" must be a problem others desire to solve.

Step 4: Outline the Specific Steps Taken

Pay attention to the exact path you followed. People pay for a process that helps them move forward, milestone by milestone.

- Instruction: List the actionable steps you took for each transformation.
- Example entries:
    - Career change: Researched new industries, took online certification, networked with professionals, updated résumé, prepared for interviews
    - Health: Created a workout schedule, meal prepped Sundays, tracked meals, set weekly goals
    - Financial: Listed all debts, created a payment plan, cut unnecessary spending, set up automatic savings

- Validation criteria: Each step should be teachable, repeatable, and lead to tangible progress.

Proving People Want Your Solution

Finding a transformation is only part of the process. To ensure your course will sell, see if people are already searching for help. Search for similar courses on Udemy or other platforms; count reviews and see what people praise or complain about. Read comment sections for frustrations or results students still want. Browse Reddit threads in relevant forums to spot recurring obstacles, and join Facebook groups to observe questions that come up again and again. Make note of frustrations that are repeated. The more you see a specific problem mentioned, the greater the demand for a proven solution.

Courses that create real results — whether it's becoming a first-time manager, learning a new language, building better habits, or simply organizing chaos — are the ones people trust with their money. If you can define a transformation based on your own experience, showing exactly how you achieved it and proving others crave the same outcome, you've already built the foundation for a profitable course. The technical steps for building a course platform are next, and anyone can master them with the right tools.

LAUNCHING, SELLING, AND SCALING YOUR COURSE ONLINE

Deciding where to host your online course is the first step in turning your knowledge into steady income. Two main types of platforms are available: course marketplaces and self-hosted platforms. Each comes with its own pros and cons, shaped by cost, technical needs, and how much control you want.

Platform Analysis

Course Marketplaces

Platforms like Udemy or Skillshare make it easy to start. They handle all the tech, process payments, and bring in traffic from their user base. The setup is typically quick, requiring only uploads of your course material. This works well for creators who want to focus on content instead of promotion. However, marketplaces often keep 50-75% of each sale as commission, so your earnings per student drop. For example, an Excel mastery course priced at $49 might earn you only $12 to $15 after fees. Marketplaces have wide exposure, but you give up control over your pricing and student information. Ongoing updates are limited, and engagement features, except for basic Q&A or community spaces, are minimal. Most courses in marketplaces sell for $20-$100, with average conversion rates around 2-4% on platform traffic. Maintenance is low, but repeat sales can be challenging unless you continually create new courses.

Self-Hosted Platforms

Sites like Teachable or Kajabi give full control over sales, branding, and pricing. You keep most of your revenue, paying only for the platform or a small transaction fee (often $30-$150/month, with some transaction fees at 2-5%). You set course prices — maybe $297 for a social media marketing program or package a painting course for $97 plus monthly membership. Self-hosting brings ownership advantages: access to student emails, better engagement tools like live chat, quizzes, or certificates, and the flexibility to link with other software. However, you're also in charge of driving traffic, which means setting up payment gateways, emails, and integrations on your own. Setup typically takes 15-30 hours. The revenue potential is higher, and average conversion rates from your own audience reach 5–8%. Ongoing updates, tech maintenance, and marketing are your responsibility.

Platform Type	Setup Time	Pricing Range	Average Commission	Control over pricing.	Typical Maintenance
Marketplace	2-5 hrs	$20-$100	50-75%	Low	Low
Self-Hosted	15-30 hrs	$97-$997+	0-5%	High	High

Revenue and Control Examples

A watercolor artist sold 800 units of a $97 painting course on Udemy in a year, but after commissions, they received roughly $9,600. Another ran the same course through Teachable, sold only 300 units, but kept 95% of each sale — netting around $27,600. A premium coaching course for careers at $1,297 hosted on Kajabi, with a 2% sales page conversion and 4,000 targeted visitors per year, can generate over $100,000, especially with a single live onboarding webinar and group access. In all cases, control over content and student data translates into better upsell capacity and recurring revenue from memberships or bundles.

Building an Automated Sales Funnel

Lead Magnet Creation

For an Excel course, offer a downloadable "Top 10 Excel Formulas" guide. Watercolor example: a free video tutorial on creating vibrant washes. Social media marketing: checklist for winning your first 100 followers. These should be immediately useful, relevant, and quick to access. Expect opt-in conversion rates of 20-40% on targeted landing page traffic.

Email Sequence Structure

Automate a simple five-to-seven email nurture sequence.

1. Welcome and deliver lead magnet
2. Story and credibility (case study or personal results)
3. Common mistakes in the field

4. Value lesson: quick win or tip
5. Invitation to webinar or mini-course
6. Overcome objections / FAQs
7. Direct sales offer with time-limited bonus

Open rates typically start at 35-45%, with 2-5% purchase rates from engaged subscribers. Setup and integration using platforms like ConvertKit take about 2–4 hours.

Webinar Framework

Host a 60-minute live or automated webinar, blending teaching with storytelling and soft selling. Use a clear agenda:

- 10 min: Introduction and personal results
- 20 min: High-value teaching
- 10 min: Mistake busting and opportunities
- 10 min: Demo of your system
- 10 min: Offer and Q&A

Webinar conversions run 6-10% if traffic is warm (from your email list).

Upsells and Integrations

After purchase, offer personal coaching, a membership, or bundled classes. Set up integrations to automatically enroll students, tag them for follow-up, and unlock bonuses. Platforms like Zapier help automate these steps.

Sustainable Revenue Models

Mix entry courses ($27-97) for wide reach, mid-tier ($197-497) for signature content, and premium ($997+) with coaching or group sessions. Bundling related classes increases transaction value by 30-50%. Add membership options for ongoing access ($29-49/month), and offer affiliate deals (20-30% commission) to expand reach.

Practical Exercise

- List your must-have platform features (commission, maintenance, engagement tools)
- Sketch out your lead magnet and email sequence for your topic
- Choose three price points for your offers
- Outline the automation steps, noting key integrations

The right decisions help turn your course into a true business asset that runs — and grows — on autopilot.

Now that we understand how to identify a compelling transformation based on our own experience and validate its demand, we can confidently create online courses that deliver real, lasting results to learners. By choosing the right platform — whether a marketplace for ease or self-hosting for greater control — and building automated sales funnels with lead magnets, email sequences, and webinars, we set the stage for scalable passive income. With thoughtful pricing strategies and ongoing engagement through upsells and memberships, turning knowledge into a sustainable business becomes not only achievable but also rewarding. This foundation empowers aspiring entrepreneurs and professionals to move beyond traditional limits and build diversified income streams with lasting impact.

ELEVEN
PROFITING FROM DIGITAL PRODUCTS AND TEMPLATES

Have you ever wondered how some entrepreneurs build thriving businesses by selling digital products that require little ongoing effort? Many begin with a simple idea — a planner, a template, or a checklist — and turn it into a reliable income stream that grows far beyond their initial investment of time. Yet for most people, knowing where to start or how to navigate crowded online marketplaces can feel overwhelming. Questions about designing appealing products, choosing the right sales platform, and reaching potential customers often stand in the way of turning ideas into profit.

This chapter will guide you through the process of developing digital products from scratch using accessible tools and efficient workflows. You'll learn how to identify market needs, design valuable offerings, and choose the best platforms to reach your audience. We'll also explore strategies for building visibility and engaging customers through email marketing, helping you grow your sales steadily while maintaining quality and brand consistency. By mastering these steps, you can create scalable digital assets that play a lasting role in your financial independence.

FROM IDEA TO CREATION: BUILDING PROFITABLE DIGITAL PRODUCTS EFFICIENTLY

Digital products are thriving due to their scalability and ease of distribution. Among the most in-demand categories, planners, templates, and printables consistently rank at the top of bestseller lists. For example, a "Social Media Content Calendar" template targets freelance marketers who struggle with consistent posting. This product can typically be created in under four hours utilizing a beginner's understanding of Google Sheets or Canva. Social media agencies and solo entrepreneurs are willing to pay $12–$25 for a ready-to-use, customizable calendar. Market demand is high, indicated by thousands of sales and positive reviews for similar items on platforms like Etsy, where related keywords show steady search volume month to month.

A "Wedding Planning Checklist" printable addresses overwhelm and forgotten details for engaged couples, especially those managing large events on their own. This printable may take two to six hours to develop using Canva or PowerPoint, requiring basic graphic and organizational skills. The typical price point is $10–$15, with high customer interest seen in recurring Etsy and Creative Market bestsellers. Customers praise checklists that break down the process into timelines and vendors, flagging "easy-to-follow" and "comprehensive" as desirable features.

Personal finance is another profitable niche, exemplified by a "Personal Budget Tracker" in Google Sheets with automated formula calculations, pie charts, and customizable monthly tabs. It solves the challenge of tracking expenses and sticking to savings goals — frequent pain points for recent graduates and young families. While more detailed than a printable, it can be developed in four to eight hours with intermediate spreadsheet skills. Price points range from $8 for basic versions to $40 for complex trackers with dashboards and tutorials. Consistent top-seller status and requests for new features in user reviews attest to high market demand.

To identify winning product ideas, research real customer behavior and competitor offerings. Start by browsing the top charts on Etsy and Creative Market. Record how often products appear, their review counts, and sales estimates where available. For deeper insight, sift through the customer reviews section and note recurring requests (such as "please add a yearly overview") or complaints ("the formulas are wrong in the March tab"). Pinterest is also a rich source for trending topics; search niche-specific terms (like "teacher lesson plan printables") and observe which pins have high engagement statistics.

Seek product gaps by comparing the features of current bestsellers with what reviews request. If dozens appreciate a meal planner but mention it's undated, this signals an opportunity to release a version with date selectors or themed variants (for example, a 12-week meal planner with weekly grocery lists, macro tracking, and links to healthy recipes).

Market Research Activity

- Select three popular products in your chosen niche.
- Create a table listing each one's features, price, and review highlights.

Product Name	Features	Price	Review Highlights
Weekly Fitness Log	Habit tracker, progress graphs	$14	"Easy to update," "Colorful"
90-Day Meal Planner	Recipe database, grocery lists	$17	"Wish it had calorie tracker"
Home Budget Sheet	Income/expense auto calc	$22	"Formulas work perfectly"

- Note three improvements you could make, such as adding color themes, integrating printable and digital formats, or including detailed user instructions.

- Outline your potential unique selling points, like "custom calorie tracking for meal plans," "auto-updating holiday budgets," or "print and digital bundle."

With product ideas validated, accessible design tools streamline creation. Canva's grid system enables clean, balanced layouts for planners and checklists, while drag-and-drop elements reduce the learning curve. Google Sheets supports complex logic with built-in formulas, making it easy to automate calculations for budget and habit trackers. PowerPoint allows batch creation of printable pages, using master slides to ensure consistency.

A step-by-step workflow supports efficient product development:

1. Validate your concept with marketplace feedback and competitor comparisons.
2. Plan the layout, using rough sketches or digital mockups on Canva.
3. Build out core content — fill in checklist steps, calendar dates, or tracker fields.
4. Select visuals such as icons, fonts, and color schemes.
5. Optimize format for print and digital delivery: test layouts for both PDF and editable files.
6. Perform quality checks such as proofreading, formula validations, and user flow reviews.

Reduce workload by outsourcing tasks like proofreading to freelancers on Upwork or hiring a graphic designer from Fiverr for custom illustrations. AI text generators like Jasper can assist with instructional content or guided prompts. Virtual assistants are available through platforms such as Belay and OnlineJobs.ph for repetitive formatting tasks. Batch produce product variations by duplicating templates and adjusting details — creating a suite of budget planners for students, families, and freelancers in one session.

The Digital Product Launch Toolkit includes step-by-step layout planners, editable style guides, and usage instruction sheets. Use the layout planner for arranging each product's sections logically. Style guides set fonts, color schemes, and brand elements for a cohesive look. Instruction sheets walk buyers through first use and common troubleshooting issues, increasing customer satisfaction and reducing support queries.

Conclude this section by choosing one researched product and using the provided planner template to design your first draft. Refine your product with the quality benchmarks outlined above, ensuring all formulas work and instructions are clear. With a completed draft in hand, you'll be ready to select the ideal marketplace and build launch momentum using email marketing, covered in the next section.

SELLING AND SCALING: PLATFORMS, VISIBILITY, AND EMAIL MARKETING FOR LASTING SUCCESS

When choosing a platform for your digital product, align your selection with your product type and long-term goals. Etsy is a strong fit for printables, digital art, and design templates — products with strong visual appeal and broad consumer interest. Gumroad attracts creators selling e-books, audio files, courses, and memberships, offering flexible pay-what-you-want pricing and robust creator communities. Payhip stands out for its simplicity and global reach, ideal for new sellers testing different digital asset types, from software to fitness plans.

Etsy deducts a 6.5% transaction fee from each sale, a 3% + $0.25 payment processing fee, and charges $0.20 per product listing. Payouts are usually made within 2–3 business days after a sale, making cash flow management predictable. Gumroad charges 10% on free accounts and 3.5% + 30¢ for paid accounts ($10/month for Pro users). Payouts via PayPal or direct deposit occur every Friday, with a two-day buffer for payment processing. Payhip strikes a balance with a 5% transaction fee on the free plan, 2% on Plus ($29/month), and 0% on Pro ($99/month), with payments processed instantly via Stripe or PayPal.

Each marketplace presents unique advantages. Etsy's mature built-in audience means instant exposure, with over 90 million active buyers reported annually, though competition can be fierce and keyword optimization critical. Gumroad supports large file uploads (up to 16GB), lets you set multiple price points, and facilitates EU VAT collection at no extra cost. However, it may not bring significant organic traffic; you'll need to drive most customers yourself. Payhip offers clean, simple storefronts, strong customization, and built-in affiliate management, but its organic traffic is lower than Etsy's ecosystem, so off-site promotion is vital.

Marketplace	Monthly Fees	Transaction Fees	Payment Processing	Features	Tech Requirements
Etsy	None	6.5% + 3%+$0.25	2–3 days	Built-in traffic, reviews, SEO tools	None (easy onboarding)
Gumroad	$0/$10	10%/$0	Every Friday	Subscriptions, analytics, VAT	Minimal (basic account setup)
Payhip	$0/$29/$99	5%/2%/0%	Instant	Customization, affiliate, memberships	Basic (easy to moderate)

To boost product visibility, leverage keyword optimization by analyzing competitor listings and high-traffic search terms using tools like Marmalead (for Etsy) or Google Trends. Place relevant primary keywords in your product title, description, and tags. An example of an optimized Etsy title: "Minimalist Budget Planner PDF – Printable Finance Tracker, A4 & Letter Size, Instant Download." Incorporate keywords naturally in your description — avoid stuffing.

Pinterest marketing is powerful, especially for visually oriented products. Create high-quality, vertical pins (1000x1500 px), adding keyword-rich descriptions. Pin consistently (at least 5 pins per week) to relevant boards, and join group boards in your niche for expanded reach. Pins with clear calls-to-action ("Download now," "Save for later") convert more browsers into buyers. Top-performing pins can drive 30–50% of total shop traffic.

Lead magnets like free digital samples, checklists, or mini-guides can capture potential buyers' emails and spark interest. Use Payhip's built-in free download feature or Gumroad's $0+ pay-what-you-want pricing as entry points, allowing customers to access your lead magnet in exchange for their email.

Traffic generation should combine organic social sharing, content marketing (e.g., publishing tutorials featuring your product), and paid ads if budget allows. Sharing customer reviews and use-case photos boosts credibility, nudging skeptical visitors toward purchase.

A robust email list enables direct customer engagement. Start by integrating opt-in forms on every product page and confirming new signups through a welcome email sequence:

- Email 1: "Welcome + your free planner download"
- Email 2: "How to get the most out of your digital planner" (with product tips)
- Email 3: "Exclusive 15% discount on your next purchase"

During product launches, send teaser emails ("Coming soon: The Ultimate Productivity Bundle") followed by a launch announcement, a benefits-focused reminder, and a last-chance scarcity message ("Sale ends in 6 hours!"). After purchase, nurture loyalty with surprise discounts or access to a VIP club. Automating sequences via ConvertKit or MailerLite saves time.

Branding is important in all marketplaces. Specializing in a niche — such as "planners for teachers" or "watercolor clipart sets" — lets you position yourself as the go-to expert, making your brand memorable. Consistent visuals, voice, and product presentation across Etsy, Gumroad, and Payhip reinforce recognition. Use a professional logo, standardized listing photos, and customer-focused copy. Craft a brand statement, such as "Empowering productivity with beautiful, easy-to-use digital tools for educators worldwide."

For standout product listings, include a gallery of lifestyle images, a demonstration video (if the platform supports it), and clear download instructions. For example, the "Student Planner Bundle" with screenshots, testimonials, and a usage tutorial led to a 22% higher conversion rate compared to text-only listings.

By following these steps and using platform metrics to monitor your progress, you steadily improve sales outcomes and build a loyal customer base.

Now that you have a clear, step-by-step understanding of how to create, launch, and sell scalable digital products using accessible tools and effective marketing strategies, you are well-equipped to turn your ideas into profitable offerings. By carefully researching market demand, leveraging user-friendly design platforms, and selecting the right online marketplaces, you can build products that meet real customer needs while minimizing effort. Coupled with strong email marketing and consistent branding, these practices lay the foundation for growing a sustainable digital business. With this knowledge in hand, you are ready to take deliberate action toward financial independence by expanding your passive income streams through digital products and online sales.

TWELVE
STACKING YOUR INCOME STREAMS AND SCALING UP

Imagine juggling several tasks at once — each demanding attention, yet none quite thriving because your focus is scattered. Many aspiring entrepreneurs and side hustlers find themselves overwhelmed trying to manage multiple income sources simultaneously, only to see limited progress and mounting frustration. The challenge lies not in creating streams of passive income but in strategically combining and managing them to build lasting wealth without burning out or losing sight of priorities.

This chapter explores how deliberate selection and careful management of income streams can transform extra earnings into a sustainable financial foundation. It discusses practical ways to use time efficiently, reinvest profits wisely, and establish systems that grow and scale over time. By understanding these principles, readers will be equipped to build a diversified portfolio of income sources that work together smoothly, enabling them to move steadily toward financial independence with clarity and control.

COMBINING AND MANAGING MULTIPLE INCOME STREAMS: STRATEGIES AND PRODUCTIVITY METHODS

Building sustainable wealth through multiple passive income streams requires a disciplined, step-by-step approach that balances ambition with practical workflow strategies. The journey always begins with deep mastery of one or two streams before expansion. When an author wants to develop lasting income, the smartest path is to focus on one area — a well-crafted eBook, for example — until royalties flow consistently and the production process feels routine. Only then should the author consider branching into audiobooks, leveraging the same manuscript and their understanding of audience preferences, or producing online courses based on the book's subject. This incremental mastery cements the workflow, prevents overwhelm, and sets the foundation for stacking new streams later on.

Smart Selection of Complementary Streams

Compatibility plays a central role when adding new income sources. Synergies amplify returns while reducing redundant effort. A real estate investor who manages rental properties often expands into Real Estate Investment Trusts (REITs). The cash flow from rentals provides hands-on experience and insight, while REITs offer a hands-off, liquid alternative. Earnings from rentals can be partially reinvested into REITs, smoothing monthly returns. Similarly, a digital content creator might begin with a successful blog. Once the blog earns $500+ per month in ad revenue, the creator can repurpose popular articles into scripts for a podcast or YouTube channel, both targeting overlapping but unique audiences.

Here's how compatible streams naturally align to form an efficient workflow:

Core Stream	Add-On Stream 1	Add-On Stream 2
eBook author	Audiobook narration	Online video course
Rental property owner	REIT investments	Property management tools
Blogger	Podcast episodes	Social media mini-guides

The table underscores how each new stream leverages the audience, content, or cash flow of the core stream.

Complementary Workflows in Action

Once comfortable with primary income streams, entrepreneurs should turn individual assets into multiple products. Take a blog post about personal finance. The creator can record a podcast episode expanding on its points, then film a short YouTube video explainer, and extract quotes and tips for Instagram and Twitter. This four-pronged output requires very little new research or ideation; each variant reaches different user demographics.

A practical scenario unfolds like this:

1. Write a detailed blog post (2,000 words)
2. Record a 15-minute podcast using the blog as a script
3. Shoot a 5-minute video highlighting the post's most actionable tips
4. Draft five social media graphics summarizing key points

With proper planning, this sequence takes no more than 10–12 hours to complete. If each channel earns at least $50 monthly in ad revenue or affiliate commissions, the combined output delivers $200 per month for work done largely upfront.

The 80/20 Rule for Expansion Decisions

Selective focus magnifies results. The 80/20 rule suggests that roughly 80% of revenue comes from 20% of efforts. Identify what to prioritize by tracking actual returns. If an author tracks book royalties, they might see that one title earns $1,000/month, while three others make only $150 each. Rather than launch more books blindly, the author analyzes why the top title performs so well — genre, promotion channel, or audience. The goal: double down on similar high-performers by investing time in proven winners or by adapting their format (e.g., creating a workbook version).

Metrics clarify decisions. Set a threshold: only pursue new ventures projected to generate at least $100/month after three months. Content creator Pat Flynn, for example, grew his passive income by focusing on podcast episodes that consistently pulled in 70% of his sponsorship revenue, cutting projects that lagged behind.

Pitfalls, Solutions, and Work-Life Harmony

Common pitfalls include burnout, overcommitment, and poor tracking. Entrepreneurs often launch too many streams at once, diluting energy and seeing stagnant results. An actionable solution is to schedule "focus sprints" — two-month periods concentrated on a single new stream while maintaining the others.

Use simple project management tools. Trello helps writers and investors track progress. Content calendars — even just a shared Google Sheet — ensure deadlines and publishing cadences remain public and actionable.

Set time boundaries. Limit deep work to three 90-minute sessions per week for new stream development. Use metrics like weekly revenue and hours invested to assess whether to continue or pivot.

Systematic Workflow and Scalability

Efficiency and scalability rely on well-documented, repeatable processes. Templates for blog posts, podcast scripts, or landlord checklists help to automate future output. Business planning apps or simple SOPs ensure that each new addition fits with, rather than overloads, the existing system. These structures make adding streams feel like puzzle pieces snapping together, rather than jigsaw chaos. Productivity and time management become not just helpful but essential as each income stream multiplies. A systematic approach is the cornerstone of building resilient, scalable passive income.

SCALING UP: REINVESTING PROFITS, BUILDING SYSTEMS, AND PLANNING FOR FINANCIAL INDEPENDENCE

Analyzing the journey from a single passive income stream to a robust wealth-generating system demands a strategic approach to reinvestment, expansion, and optimization. Begin by earmarking 50% of net profits each month for reinvestment. Divide this allocation into two main buckets: 30% into low-cost index funds and 20% into Real Estate Investment Trusts (REITs), leveraging platforms like Vanguard (for index funds) and Fundrise (for REITs). Reserve another 20% for business growth tools such as ConvertKit for email marketing and Zapier for workflow automation. This structure creates a flywheel that builds long-term stability. Retain the remaining 30% as liquid reserves for flexibility or potential new ventures. Criteria for launching additional products should hinge on consistent month-over-month growth of at least 20% and a recurring profit margin above 30%. For example, if your dropshipping store hits this milestone for four consecutive months, allocate a portion of profits to explore adjacent niches or develop complementary digital products.

Momentum building is measured by establishing core metrics that clarify when to expand. Set a monthly minimum passive revenue goal. When a stream regularly brings in $1,000 in net monthly passive income with at least a 40% ROI (which is found by dividing net profit by total invested capital), it shows that it is ready to grow. Add dashboards that track customer acquisition cost (CAC), churn rate (if applicable), and lifetime value (LTV). Doubling down becomes the logical next step when CAC decreases while LTV and retention increase. For instance, if shifting 10% of the marketing budget from ads to affiliate partners boosts profits by 15%, that's a clear signal to reinvest more heavily in affiliate outreach.

Brand growth accelerates through targeted digital infrastructure upgrades. Start with a full website audit using tools like SEMrush or Ahrefs to eliminate slow-loading elements, fix broken links, and enhance on-page SEO. Integrate heatmap analytics — such as Hotjar — to identify high-engagement areas for optimized product placement or content upgrades. For newsletters, use MailerLite or ConvertKit to segment lists by customer interests, automate nurture sequences, and implement A/B tests for subject lines. Launch a biweekly value-driven newsletter packed with actionable tips, curated resources, and community spotlights. In community building, nurture engagement through private Facebook groups or Discord servers. Assign moderators, schedule weekly themed discussions, and incentivize contributor-generated content with monthly contests. These steps deepen audience loyalty and amplify organic reach.

Wealth measurement benefits from tangible autonomy metrics and scorecards. Define financial independence as covering core monthly living expenses (including housing, food, insurance, and personal savings) through passive streams. Use a "Freedom Scorecard" to track milestones: 25%, 50%, 75%, and 100% coverage. Create a table to map income streams to expense categories, helping spot areas for improvement. Balance financial goals with lifestyle by setting quarterly reviews to assess time spent on business maintenance versus leisure. Set a rule that major business decisions should not encroach beyond 20 hours of active engagement per month once mature systems are in place.

Robust Standard Operating Procedures (SOPs) enable the business to become systematized. Use tools like Notion or Google Docs to template every recurring task — listing product research steps, customer support responses, and content publishing schedules. Develop visual workflows for automations, such as connecting Shopify sales to Printful order fulfillment and Xero bookkeeping via Zapier. In digital product businesses, automate email delivery, license generation, and customer follow-ups. For content platforms, schedule posts with

Buffer or Hootsuite. Each process needs a clear trigger, action, and defined outcome for scalability.

Outsourcing demands a cost-benefit evaluation for every potential hire. Calculate the hourly cost of your time, then compare it to rates on platforms like Upwork for virtual assistants, copywriters, or technical specialists. If your time is valued at $80/hour and a VA charges $15/hour, delegating 10 hours/week immediately recaptures 65% of that value. Draft job descriptions listing required skills, daily tasks, preferred tools, and KPIs (key performance indicators). Use scorecards to assess new hires on criteria like responsiveness, accuracy, and initiative. For remote team management, adopt frameworks like daily Slack check-ins, weekly Asana project reviews, and monthly Zoom strategy sessions.

Exit strategies require understanding asset value. Digital businesses are commonly valued at 30–45x average monthly net profit. To sell a blog generating $2,000/month, a typical range is $60,000–$90,000. Explore licensing your brand, content, or digital products with clear royalty structures (e.g., 10% of gross sales) and defined term lengths. Decide on the optimum scale for an exit by monitoring peak profitability and market trends, ensuring you sell during heightened demand or automation maturity.

Continuous reinvestment and compounding returns lie at the heart of the wealth flywheel. Even modest annual growth rates — 10%–12% — turn $10,000 into over $31,000 in ten years. Chart your "time-to-freedom" based on expenses replaced by passive streams, noting each milestone when a new stream covers another core cost. This creates a living scoreboard motivating consistent effort and smart decisions on the path to sustainable, automated, and freeing wealth.

Now that we know how to effectively combine and manage different sources of passive income by mastering them, reinvesting wisely, and using efficient systems, we can confidently create a lasting way to achieve financial freedom. By thoughtfully selecting complementary income sources, applying disciplined time management, and leveraging automation and outsourcing, aspiring entrepreneurs can scale their wealth while maintaining balance and clarity. This chapter lays the foundation for expanding income with intention, reinforcing that true financial independence comes from steady growth, careful planning, and continuous optimization — empowering readers to take deliberate steps toward lasting prosperity beyond the constraints of traditional work.

HELP THE NEXT DREAMER BREAK FREE

Every insight we share can become a **stepping stone** for someone else searching for *freedom*.

Have you ever wished you had a *trusted guide* when trying to break free from the endless cycle of **trading time for money**?

Picture an aspiring entrepreneur, a burned-out professional, or a parent longing for *more time with their family* — someone who knows there must be a better way but feels overwhelmed by all the noise online. Your reflections on ***Passive Income Mastery*** could give them the clarity and courage to take their *first step*.

If this book helped you **understand passive income more clearly**, *sparked an idea* for your first income stream, or inspired you to think bigger about your financial future, I'd be honored if you would leave a short, honest review.

Your feedback not only supports my work — it also guides future readers who may be standing right where you once stood, *uncertain but hopeful*. Even a few sentences can **ripple outward**, helping others find the tools and confidence they need to reclaim their time and build *real freedom*.

Thank you for reading, reflecting, and sharing your journey. **Your words carry more power than you may realize.**

CONCLUSION

As you reach the end of this book, pause for a moment and reflect on the journey you have begun. The pursuit of passive income is not reserved for the fortunate few, nor is it a speculative gamble reserved for risk-takers. Rather, it is a disciplined, empowering process that anyone — with determination and commitment — can undertake. The blueprint is now in your hands, but its power lies in your willingness to act upon it. Passive income is not about chasing a fantasy of instant riches or abandoning all structure overnight; instead, it is about building enduring assets, step by step, until your money works harder than you do. It is the transformation from striving to thriving, from simply earning to consciously creating a life that serves your purpose and ambitions.

At the core of this approach is a profound shift in mindset. Many adults have been conditioned to see themselves exclusively as consumers or employees, bound to trade hours for dollars and to wait for others to set the limits of their financial destiny. This book has challenged you to reframe that narrative. You are invited to become a creator — to invest time and ideas into ventures that generate value long after your initial effort. You are encouraged to evolve into an investor — someone who sees opportunities where others see uncertainty and who builds systems and assets rather than watching passively from the sidelines. Most importantly, you are learning to transition from earning for survival to building a future where you can reclaim your time, direct your energy, and choose how you live every day.

Let us briefly revisit the path you have traveled throughout these chapters. In the early pages, you laid a critical foundation by identifying your "why" — the deeper motivation behind your desire for passive income — and clarifying your specific financial goals. This goal-setting process was more than a box to check; it was an act of taking ownership over your life's trajectory. With this clarity, you began constructing the scaffolding on which all subsequent actions would rest.

You've now explored a wide range of income streams, uncovering real-world strategies, analyzing risks and rewards, and reviewing practical steps for implementation. Whether you were drawn to the steady returns of dividend-paying stocks, the creative potential of digital products, the transformative opportunities in crypto assets, or the timeless wealth-building power of real estate, one truth became clear: there's no single formula for freedom. Each asset class comes with its own advantages and demands. You gained insights into earning royalties from intellectual property and content revenue, examined how to automate and scale online businesses, and explored emerging trends that are redefining how people earn beyond hourly wages. Across all these paths, one theme remained constant: lasting wealth and autonomy depend on building assets that continue to pay you — even while your focus shifts elsewhere.

The final section equipped you with advanced concepts necessary for sustained growth — how to stack multiple streams, scale them intelligently, and automate processes to minimize ongoing effort. Here, true freedom comes into view, not just as a financial state, but as a holistic transformation of daily living. Diverse, resilient portfolios protect your income from market shifts and personal setbacks alike, while automation and outsourcing free up space for creativity, relationships, and meaningful pursuits.

As you close this book, remember that there are infinite ways to build passive income, each uniquely suited to your strengths, interests, and circumstances. There is no universal right answer — only the path that aligns with your skills, resources, and vision for your ideal lifestyle. Whether you thrive on writing, coding, investing, teaching, or building communities, the modern economy offers countless entry points for generating lasting, automated wealth. Your job now is not to seek perfection or certainty but to select a single starting point and give it concrete shape.

Action must follow intention. Perhaps you have long dreamed of publishing your knowledge in an ebook, launching a video channel, acquiring your first rental property, or purchasing a basket of dividend stocks. Now is the time to commit to that first step. Create your outline. Record your introduction. Open an investment account. Begin researching your target market. Progress, not perfection, will propel you forward. Every imperfect first step sets the stage for incremental growth. Momentum emerges not from inaction, but from small wins repeated consistently over time. Let repetition become your ally as you refine your processes and expand your portfolio. Obstacles and setbacks are natural; resilience is developed through action and reflection, not hesitation.

Do not underestimate what is at stake in your decision to pursue passive income. At its heart, this blueprint is not merely a financial strategy — it is a means to reclaim agency over your most precious asset: time. Imagine mornings that begin gently, without alarm clocks dictating your routine. Envision the flexibility to travel widely, pursue creative passions, or spend time with loved ones, unencumbered by the requirement to ask permission or schedule vacation days. Imagine yourself contributing to causes you care about, confident that self-sustaining assets are meeting your essential needs in the background. Passive income is about unlocking options, reducing stress, and amplifying your impact on your terms.

Throughout this process, keep sight of your original purpose — your freedom number, the tangible milestone that represents both security and possibility. That number may signify the chance to leave a draining job, support a family, or simply regain balance between work and life. Whatever your unique aspiration, let it guide your decisions and reinforce your commitment during challenging moments. Each step, however incremental, moves you closer to that vision of independence and fulfillment.

Finally, remember that the journey toward financial freedom does not have to be lonely. Countless others are charting similar paths, experimenting with new models, and overcoming obstacles by sharing experiences and insights. You are invited to connect with like-minded individuals, leverage resource hubs, and contribute your voice to communities dedicated to sustainable wealth-building. Stay engaged by joining our newsletter, accessing free tools, and participating in forums designed to keep you accountable and inspired. Nothing accelerates progress like mutual encouragement and shared learning. Share your journey openly, for your story may inspire someone else to begin their transformation.

The blueprint is in your possession. Every principle, tool, and strategy outlined in these pages is ready to serve you. Do not let fear or uncertainty delay your pursuit of freedom. Take a bold first step today. Keep learning, keep building, and keep stacking your income streams until you have not only achieved your goals but surpassed them.

You've got the blueprint. Now build the life no one can take from you.

SSI
COME
ER

Made in the USA
Monee, IL
04 November 2026

67384795R00069